ROME
and the Vatican

*An illustrated guide to Rome's art,
culture, monuments, traditions, and cuisine*

Publication created and designed by: *Casa Editrice Bonechi.* Editorial management: *Monica Bonechi.*
Graphics, image research and video pagemaking: *Serena de Leonardis.*
Cover: *Manuela Ranfagni.* Drawings: *Stefano Benini.* Editing: *Anna Baldini, Federica Balloni, Elena Rossi.*
Additional English translations: *Paula E. Boomsliter. Texts compiled by the Casa Editrice Bonechi
Editorial Department;* texts on pages 60-61 and 118-127 by *Maria Novella Batini.*

Printed in Italy by *Centro Stampa Editoriale Bonechi, Sesto Fiorentino.*

The photographs property of the *Casa Editrice Bonechi* archives are the work of:
*Marco Banti, Gaetano Barone, Emanuela Crimini, Gianni Dagli Orti, Andrea Fantauzzo, Paolo Giambone,
Dario Grimoldi, Nicola Grifoni, Serena de Leonardis, Foto M.S.A., Stefano Masi, Andrea Pistolesi,
Gustavo Tomsich, Cesare Tonini, Michele Tonini.*
The following photographers also contributed to this publication:
Art Archive/Gianni Dagli Orti: p. 107 top right, 108 bottom right, 109 bottom.
Maria Novella Batini: p. 58, 59, 60 center and bottom, 61, 64 top to bottom right, 66 bottom, 126 bottom.
Foto Archivio Fabbrica di San Pietro in Vaticano: p. 75 top, 77 top.
Foto Musei Vaticani: p. 85, 86 bottom, 86/87 top, 88/89 top (*P. Abbrescia*), 88/89 bottom, 90, 91 top and bottom
(A. Brachetti, P. Zigrossi), 91 center (*P. Zigrossi*). *Foto Pont. Comm. Arch. Sacra:* p. 115. *Foto Scala:* p. 51.
Francesco Giannoni: p. 4 top, 11 top, 39 top, 46 center, 54, 83 bottom, 105 bottom, 111 top right and bottom,
116. *Andrea Jemolo:* p. 1, 10 top and bottom, 12, 23 top, 24, 40 bottom, 42 bottom, 44 top, 46 top, 47 top, 50, 52
bottom, 55 top, 83 top, 84, 94 top left, 95, 97 bottom, 100 top, 101 bottom, 102 top. *Leonardo Olmi:*
p. 28-29 bottom, 72-73, 118-119. *Eliana Pallisco:* p. 20, 27. *Giuliano Valsecchi:* p. 14 top right.
Arnaldo Vescovo: p. 105 top, 110 top.

The publisher apologizes for any unintentional omissions, and would be pleased to
include appropriate acknowledgements in any subsequent edition of this publication.

www.bonechi.com
ISBN 978-88-476-1700-1

THE CITY THROUGH THE CENTURIES

Rome is one of a very few cities in the world that can boast 3000 years of uninterrupted civilization. Variously called Caput mundi, Eternal City, *and "capital of the ancient western world and capital of Christendom," legend sets the date of its founding, in a strategic position for trade on the Palatine hill in proximity to the Tiber river and the sea, at 753 BC—but the site has revealed traces of a settlement of farmers/herders from the 14th-10th century BC.*

From Enclave on the Tiber to Eternal City

Rome's legendary beginnings were followed by the celebrated period of the seven kings of Rome, during which the primitive village expanded and strengthened. The Roman Republic was established in 509 BC, and with it came the final decline of Etruscan civilization: the city on the Tiber was destined to last. Reinforced during the glorious eras of the Republic and the Empire, with possessions beyond the English Channel, throughout the Mediterranean basin, and as far east as the Persian Gulf, the Eternal City survived the tumultuous period of the barbarian invasions. Rome was reborn in the 15th century ca. and flourished as capital of the Papal States; in 1871, it Rome became capital of the united Kingdom of Italy and in 1946 of the Republic of Italy.

The Many Faces of Rome

Even a cursory glance at the city from the Capitoline hill reveals the many faces of this great Mediterranean metropolis, caressed by the winds of the not-far-off sea, and provides an outline of its history. From **archaeological** Rome of the ancient ruins to Rome the **papal capital** of the striking vistas: the parks inside and beyond the walls, the facades of the **Renaissance** and **Baroque** palaces, the squares that open unexpectedly in the intricate fabric of narrow **medieval** streets. Age-old buildings with shady courtyards and eternally-flowering terraces are host at street level to **coffee shops** and **trattorie** where the daily lives of Rome's citizens intersect the worlds of tourism, politics, art, and cinema, with its glorious capital, **Cinecittà**, Hol-

lywood. In many city **quarters**, like San Lorenzo or Trastevere, framed by the venerable churches of Santa Maria and Santa Cecilia, and in the **squares** and the **markets**, we come face to face with the Rome of the Romans: a warm, hospitable city, the ancient *caput mundi* with its natural cosmopolitan vocation and a great modern city resting on thirty centuries of history. A visit to the **Vatican** will show us the grandeur of the heart of pontifical Rome and **artistic treasures** of peerless beauty, from Michelangelo's *Pietà* to the Sistine Chapel, the Vatican Museums, Saint Peter's Basilica, and the Colonnade in Saint Peter's Square. In the 20th century, the city acquired **new quarters**, some monumental, like the EUR, home of important public institutions and museums, which grew up from 1938 to well after 1950 along the road leading to the sea at Ostia. Not far away is the popular Garbatella district, a garden city built in the 1920s on a hilly site, where fine period homes alternate with the green of trees and gardens.

Detail of the portal by Cecco Bonanotte at the new entrance to the Vatican Museums.

The original bronze statue of Marcus Aurelius in the Capitoline Museums.

Ancient Rome

Anyone's first visit to Rome will start from its heart, the **Capitoline**, the most important of the famed seven hills: dear to the Romans as a sacred site in antiquity and later, down through modern times, as the seat of city government, in the form conceived in the 1500s by Michelangelo. The hill offers a sweeping panorama of the city, the valley hosting the **Colosseum** and the facing Palatine hill. The ruins of Rome's forums narrate daily life and business in the Republican and Imperial ages: below the Capitoline is the **Roman Forum**; stretching alongside the hill, the **Imperial Forums**, culminating in Trajan's column and recently the site of new excavations.

At the foot of the hill, near the Tiber, the archaeological area continues with the Theater of Marcellus and through the Porticus of Octavia into the suggestive Ghetto quarter. The **Palatine** hill is the cradle of Roman civilization; alongside majestic ruins from the Imperial age, the area preserves testimony of the remote origins of the Eternal City. It was in Imperial times—and in particular under the first emperor, Augustus (27 BC - 14 AD)—that ancient Rome achieved its maximum splendor, with baths, temples, colonnades, triumphal arches, and the forums, the largest Roman monumental complex to have come down to us. The common people lived in true multi-story "apartment buildings". The entire city was completely transformed. Wood and brick were replaced by materials destined to survive through the centuries: durable marble and other stones, and in particular **travertine**, are found almost everywhere in Rome, a unifying note that lends the city a special light all its own.

After the glories of the Imperial age, Rome was thrown into the Dark Ages by the barbarian incursions and seemed unaware of the archeological treasures preserved under its surface while livestock grazed on the Capitoline and among the half-buried ruins of the forums. With the rediscovery and the

Capitoline Hill

Fontana di Trevi

Colosseum

rise of the cult of the classical world, in the 1700s, Rome became a source of inspiration for paintings and prints and a destination of choice for European nobles and artists, who completed their education among the ancient vestiges of the Eternal City; and above all, the city was studied by the **archaeologists** who laid the foundations for systematic excavations that began in the 19th century and are still evolving.

Medieval Rome

The oldest Roman churches reveal important information about Rome in the Middle Ages. In the 4th century, thanks to the advent of **Christianity**, the city succeeded in ferrying the critical period of the decline of the Empire and the first barbarian invasions. Moving in the direction mapped out by Constantine (emperor from 303 to 327)—who granted Christians freedom to worship and the Roman Catholic church, possession of the city—the new religion consecrated Rome as the seat of its Church and launched it as the new **spiritual guide of the western world**. This function was reinforced when Charlemagne was crowned first emperor of the Holy Roman Empire on Christmas day in the year 800. Testimony to Christian Rome is offered by the so-called **Constantinian basilicas** (*San Giovanni in Laterano, San Pietro in Vaticano, Santa Maria Maggiore, San Paolo fuori le Mura*), of 4th-century origin, and the numerous 5th-century early Christian churches, such as *Santa Maria in Trastevere,* although these buildings have come down to us only through long series of restoration work and stylistic revisitations. In the 7th century, the heart of the city was demolished and rebuilt using materials scavenged from the ancient Roman constructions, and the pagan temples—like the *Pantheon*—were transformed into Christian churches. The cloisters of *San Giovanni in Laterano* and *San Paolo fuori le Mura* contain notable examples of an important development in medieval sacred art best represented

The interior of the Pantheon.

Below, from top to bottom:
Trinità dei Monti, Castel Sant'Angelo, San Pietro.

Arch of Constantine

San Giovanni in Laterano

5

The Fontana di Trevi.

A view of Palazzo Farnese.

Bottom, a detail of the 13th-century frescoes in Santa Cecilia in Trastevere and the Cosmatesque decor in the basilica of San Paolo fuori le Mura.

the ruins of the Theater of Marcellus.

From the Quattrocento to Modern-day Rome

The Capitoline slope opposite that facing on the Roman Forum—the fulcrum of the Classical age—looks toward the Vatican and **monumental Rome**, at the foot of the hill, between Piazza Venezia and Piazza del Popolo, furrowed by the straight line of Via del Corso. Since the early Middle Ages, the history of the city has been indissolubly linked to the history of the pontifical state: with the return of the pope to the Vatican in 1376, following the exile of the papacy to Avignon, Rome once again became a vital crossroads for culture and trade. Stimulated by the now more powerful Church, the city flowered during the 15th century. Rome was reborn mostly at the hand of artists from other regions, in the main from the cradle of the artistic Renaissance, Tuscany. Invited by illuminated pontiffs—among whom Sixtus IV, who commissioned Botticelli, Perugino, Pinturicchio, Signorelli, and Ghirlandaio to produce the *Sistine Chapel* wall frescoes— artists of the caliber of Donatello, Lorenzo Ghiberti, and Leon Battista Alberti flocked to the papal court. "Must sees" from this period are elegant *Palazzo Venezia*, the first great example of Renaissance civil architecture, *Palazzo della Cancelleria*, attributed in part to Bramante, *Santa*

by the creations of the **Cosmati family**. The Cosmatis were masters in the art of mosaic decoration, which they applied to bishops' thrones, ambones, portals, tortile columns, and floors, using marble and other recovered materials. The religious buildings of the Communal period are characterized by their

Romanesque style. In the field of civil architecture, the tower-homes reflected the struggles among noble families for control of the city's various quarters, while a number of ancient Roman buildings were transformed into patrician residences; an outstanding example of this trend is Palazzo Orsini, which rose on

Maria del Popolo, San Pietro in Montorio, with Bramante's celebrated Tempietto, and finally what is considered the most sublime expression of 16th-century Roman architecture: *Palazzo Farnese*, by Giuliano da Sangallo the Younger but with additions by Michelangelo. The greatest artistic creations of the Roman Cinquecento date to the reign of Pope Julius II: the *decoration of the ceiling and end wall of the Sistine Chapel*, both by Michelangelo, and the *Raphael Rooms*.

The 17th century saw the triumph of the style that typically connotes the Roman cityscape, the **Baroque**. Caravaggio dominated in the field of painting, while Francesco Borromini and Gianlorenzo Bernini vied for first place in architecture. Borromini created the daring forms of *Sant'Ivo alla Sapienza*, while Bernini designed the solemn *colonnade in Saint Peter's Square* and was an artist of inexhaustible energy in the field of statuary, of which the *Galleria Borghese* contains numerous examples. This was the age of important **urban renovation works** that gave Rome the grandiose aspect for which it is renowned worldwide: from *Saint Peter's Square* to *Piazza Navona, Piazza di Spagna* with the *Spanish Steps*, and *Via del Corso*, which cuts through the heart of the monumental city. In Rome's "golden age," from the 15th to the 17th century, the city confirmed the vocation it still professes: Rome is a city more than capable of changing its face without losing its identity, a city in continual evolution, a city that can welcome and integrate all that is new into that stratified cultural terrain that is its great strength and a touchstone of equilibrium and harmony. Proclamation of **Rome as capital** of the Kingdom of Italy (1871) led to further intervention in the heart of the medieval city; the most significant is the thoroughfare composed of Via Nazionale and Corso Vittorio Emanuele that links the railroad terminus with the **Capitoline** and, on the other side of the Tiber, the **Vatican**.

The spiral ramp at the new entrance to the Vatican Museums.

Villa Borghese.

The Auditorium of the Parco della Musica entertainment venue by Renzo Piano.

CAPITOLINE HILL

From the earliest times, the Capitoline hill (or Campidoglio) was the center of the political, social, and religious life of Rome. Its summit is now crowned by Michelangelo's Piazza del Campidoglio, defined by illustrious palaces and magnificently decorated with the statue of Marcus Aurelius set at the center

of the intriguing interplay of ellipses and volutes designed by Michelangelo for the grey pavement of the square. Formerly in Piazza di San Giovanni in Laterano, Marcus Aurelius was moved to the Campidoglio in 1538: apparently, Michelangelo had not previously taken the statue into consideration as decoration for the square.

PALAZZO SENATORIO

This building stands on a site on which functions linked to the political life of the city have always been carried on. It was originally that of the *Tabularium*, an impressive building housing the state archives, ordered built

in 78 BC. In 1143, work began for construction of a new building on the ruins of the *Tabularium*. In 1160 the college of senators was already meeting in the halls of the new building but the building took on its modern-day look only under Pope Paul III, who charged Michelangelo with redesigning it.

Piazza del Campidoglio with the copy of the equestrian statue of Marcus Aurelius at its center. Top, the statue of *Minerva (Dea Roma)* at the base of Palazzo Senatorio's double staircase.

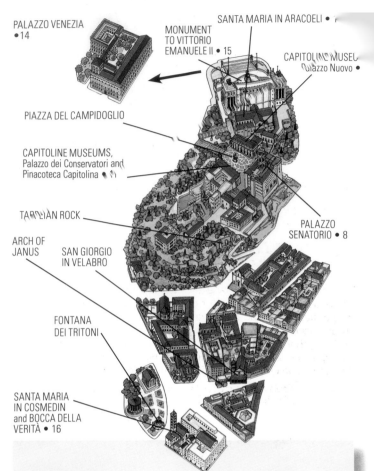

PALAZZO VENEZIA
• 14

MONUMENT
TO VITTORIO
EMANUELE II • 15

SANTA MARIA IN ARACOELI •

CAPITOLINE MUSEU
Palazzo Nuovo •

PIAZZA DEL CAMPIDOGLIO

CAPITOLINE MUSEUMS,
Palazzo dei Conservatori and
Pinacoteca Capitolina •

TARPEIAN ROCK

PALAZZO
SENATORIO • 8

ARCH OF
JANUS

SAN GIORGIO
IN VELABRO

FONTANA
DEI TRITONI

SANTA MARIA
IN COSMEDIN
and BOCCA DELLA
VERITÀ • 16

The Tarpeian Rock and the Capitoline Geese

The long history of the Capitoline is constellated with events real and legendary, and many of the narrations have to do its tactical role in ancient Rome. It is told how, in 390 BC when the Gauls led by Brennus laid siege to Rome, the Capitoline geese, sacred to Juno who was worshipped here with Jupiter and Minerva (the so-called Capitoline triad) were the only animals in the city to have escaped slaughter by the famished citizens. When the Gauls attempted to take the citadel on the Capitoline hill, at the first suspicious noise the geese began to honk and alarmed the former consul Marcus Manlius, leader of the garrison on the hill, who went down in history as the man who saved the Capitol. The name of the Tarpeian Rock (*rupes Tarpeia*) recalls the myth of Tarpeia, daughter of Spurius Tarpeius, custodian of the citadel on the hill, who opened the gates to the besieging Sabines, believing she would be rewarded with gold and jewels. Instead, on entering the citadel, the Sabines suffocated Tarpeia before throwing her body over the cliff. In ancient Rome, the cruel punishment inflicted on condemned traitors was to be flung from the height to their deaths.

Top, an overall view of the exhibition hall in the Capitoline Museums' Roman Garden.

The original of the bronze equestrian statue of Marcus Aurelius following restoration and, bottom, a detail of the head.

CAPITOLINE MUSEUMS

The Capitoline Museum complex hosts one of the world's oldest and most prestigious public collections of art. It contains above all statues of the Classical era, some of which are of considerable historical-artistic importance and worldwide fame. The collections are housed in the Palazzo Nuovo and the facing Palazzo dei Conservatori, which includes the Pinacoteca Capitolina. Of note among the most recent restructuring work is renovation of the areas of the museum dedicated to the temple of Capitoline Jupiter and the new, light and airy glassed-in area that is now home to the original of the equestrian statue of Marcus Aurelius. The space features a special microclimate suitable for best preserving the celebrated statue and fragments of the bronze colossus of Constantine. The Tabularium leading in to the state archives of the ancient city has also now been opened to the public.

PALAZZO NUOVO

In 1734, Palazzo Nuovo became the first home of the Capitoline Museums. The building houses some of the most interesting examples of Roman statuary, and boasts one of the most complete collections of Imperial portraiture. The so-called **Room of the Emperors** in fact contains 65 *busts of Roman emperors* arranged in chronological order around an evocative statue of the *Seated Helena* in which the head of Constantine's mother is set on the body of a 5th-century BC Greek original. Other works on display on the halls of Palazzo Nuovo include the famous *Capitoline Venus*, a Roman copy of a Hellenistic original, the *Wounded Amazon* and the *Dying Galatian*, unearthed in the Horti Sallustian together with the *Galatian Killing his Wife* which is today in the Palazzo Altemps Museum.

Details of the remaining fragments of the colossus of Constantine.

PALAZZO DEI CONSERVATORI AND THE PINACOTECA CAPITOLINA

Since the Middle Ages the seat of one of the most important city magistratures, the **Palazzo dei Conservatori** was completely restructured to Michelangelo's plans beginning in 1563. The original destination of the palace is evident in the splendid Sale dei Conservatori, which are now used as exhibit space for some of the most celebrated of the works in the Capitoline collections: for example, the *Spinario* and the *She-Wolf (Lupa Capitolina)*, a marvelous bronze from the 5th century BC. The twins, quite probably the work of Antonio del Pollaiolo, were added in the 15th century when the statue was raised to the status of symbol of the city. The large glassed hall created by covering the Roman Garden is home to suggestive fragments, including the head and one hand, of the colossal **statue of Constantine**, moved here from the apse of the Basilica of Maxentius. Another emperor, **Marcus Aurelius**, also figures among the masterpieces on display in this exhibition space. His gilded bronze statue, believed in the Middle Ages to be the image of Constantine (and only for this reason not condemned to destruction) became a model for the equestrian monuments of the Renaissance. The museum as such is housed in the rooms and galleries of one of the wings of the palace, and contains such masterpieces as the bust of the *Emperor Commo-*

Medusa
by Gianlorenzo Bernini.

Discobolus
by Myron.

dus, the *Esquiline Venus*, the *Warrior Hercules* and the *Punishment of Marsyas*, found together with other statues in the Lamiani Gardens and the gardens of Maecenas' villa on the Esquiline. The **Castellani collection**, which includes many black- and red-figured Greek vases, is a very interesting section of this museum, which continues on into the **Braccio Nuovo** and the **Museo Nuovo**. During reorganization of the latter exhibit space, much attention was paid to the reconstruction of

Saint John the Baptist by Caravaggio.

those sculptural groups that once adorned public and sacred buildings in ancient Rome. The museum itinerary is brought to a close with the **Pinacoteca Capitolina**, established in 1748 in the other wing of the palace by Benedict XIV. His primary intention was to provide a home for the numerous paintings belonging to the Sacchetti collection and to that of Pio di Savoia. Among the many important works on exhibit here are paintings by Titian, Tintoretto, and Guido Reni, as well as the celebrated *Saint John the Baptist* by Caravaggio. A separate Capitoline Museums exhibition space has been set up in the former **Centrale Montemartini power plant.**

The statues of the two *Dioscuri* at the top of the monumental staircase that leads up to Piazza del Campidoglio. Bottom, the church of Santa Maria d'Aracoeli.

Michelangelo and Palazzo Senatorio - Michelangelo directed the work of building the **staircase** personally; it was later decorated by order of Sixtus V with the statue of the goddess *Roma Capitolina*, originally *Minerva*, in the center niche, and those of the *Nile* and the *Tiber* (originally the *Tigris*), brought to the Capitoline from the Baths of Constantine on the Quirinal hill, in those on each side. The work planned by Michelangelo was completed, with some liberties taken, between 1582 and 1605 by Giacomo della Porta, Girolamo Rainaldi, and Martino Longhi the Elder.

CHURCH OF SANTA MARIA IN ARACOELI

Mention of the church is made as early as the 7th century; in the 10th century it became a Benedictine abbey and then passed to the Friars Minor, who saw to its reconstruction around 1320. A place for associative life as well as a place of worship, the church continued in this unique calling into the 16th century: for example, the civic victory ceremony celebrating Marcantonio Colonna's victory at Lepanto (1571) was held here in 1571. In the **interior**, the Bufalini Chapel, in the right aisle, contains the *frescoes* by *Pinturicchio* that are considered his masterpieces.

Today's **Museo di Palazzo Venezia** overflows into the rooms of the adjoining Palazzetto Venezia, which communicates with the main building through the so-called "Passetto" or Corridor of the Cardinals, an ancient guard-walk modified in the eighteenth century, and houses rich collections of art including some pieces from the collection of Athanasius Kircher: terra-cotta and pottery, porcelain, bronze and silver objects, church ornaments and vestments, wooden sculptures, paintings, weapons, ivory, crystal, tapestries and objets d'art of the most disparate types, both Italian and foreign.

Museo di Palazzo Venezia: 16th-century polychrome wooden statue and *Double Portrait* by Giorgione.

PALAZZO VENEZIA

In about the mid-15th century, Cardinal Paolo Barbo began work for the construction of his residence. During the pontificate of Paul II Barbo, the building, which had incorporated in its architectural fabric the adjoining **Saint Mark's Basilica**,

the facade of which was redesigned by Alberti, underwent considerable modification: the wing which was to become the **Palazzetto Venezia** was added along Via del Plebiscito, and in the interior there was created the famous **Sala del Mappamondo**, probably decorated by Mantegna, which hosted Mussolini's cabinet during the Fascist era. In the early 16th century, Cardinal Lorenzo Cybo enlarged the Pauline layout and made further modifications to it with the creation of the so-called Cybo Apartment, which between 1564 and 1797 was home to the cardinals of San Marco. During the same period the palace was the property of the Republic of Venice, which used it as the residence of its ambassadors and further modified the original fifteenth-century structure. Still further remodeling was carried out during the two centuries that followed, until in 1924, following lengthy restoration of questionable value, the building became a museum and, from 1929 onward, the seat of the Gran Consiglio of the Fascist government.

MONUMENT TO VITTORIO EMANUELE II

Following an extenuating competition, the commission for the monument to the first king of united Italy was entrusted to Giuseppe Sacconi. It was begun in 1885, and finished and inaugurated in 1911. The theme of the building (the *"Vittoriano"*) was celebration of the splendor of the nation after the Unification of Italy with the solemn statue of *Rome* standing watch over the **Tomb of the Unknown Soldier**. Note should also be taken of the decidedly classicistic *equestrian statue of Vittorio Emmanuele II*, an integral part of the monument, as are the fateful words from the Bulletin of Victory of 4 November 1918 carved in the stone of the last level. The entrance to the **Museo Sacrario delle Bandiere della Marina Militare** is on the left side.

Facing page, a view of Palazzo Venezia.
The "Vittoriano" monument to Vittorio Emanuele II.

The interior of the Mamertine Prison: on the left, the column to which
Saint Peter was reputedly chained.

MAMERTINE PRISON

Under the church of San
Giuseppe dei Falegnami, on
the slopes of the Capitoline hill
north of the Temple of Concord,
is the "prison" given the name
"Mamertine" in the Middle
Ages. A modern entrance leads
into a trapezoidal chamber dating to the mid-2nd century BC.
A door, now walled up, led into
the other rooms of the prison,
called *latomie* because they were
adapted from the tufa quarries. A
circular opening in the pavement
of this room was originally the
only entrance to an underground
chamber where those condemned
to death and enemies of the State
were tortured and killed, generally by strangulation. According to
later Christian legend, it was here
Saint Peter was held a prisoner.

Bocca della Verità

At the back of the left side of the portico of the church of **Santa Maria in
Cosmedin** is a large stone disk representing the frowning face of a river god,
commonly known as the Bocca della Verità or "Mouth
of Truth." Although it is actually an antique drain
cover carved in the form of a mask with an
open mouth, the plaque is traditionally held
to be an incorruptible judge: those acting in
good faith can put their hands in the mouth
of the god without fear, but those whose
consciences are not quite as spotless and
who challenge the judgement of the god
run the risk of seeing the mouth snap shut
and finding their hands amputated.

ROMAN FORUM

Situated in the depression surrounded by the Palatine, the Capitoline and the Esquiline hills, the area was originally most inhospitable, swampy and unhealthy, until the surprisingly modern reclamation work carried out by king Tarquinius Priscus provided the area with a highly-developed drainage system. Once this complex reclamation work was finished, the Roman Forum became a place for trade and barter. Numerous shops and a large market square were built. An area was also set apart for public ceremonies: it was here that the magistrates were elected, the traditional religious holidays were kept, and those charged with various crimes were judged by a court with all the forensic appurtenances. After various transformations, the Roman Forum became so large as to be considered the secular, religious and commercial center of the city in Augustus' time. With the decline of the Roman Empire, the splendid but venerable structures of the forum were severely damaged during the barbarian invasions, especially those of the Goths (410 AD) and of the Vandals (455 AD). The Roman Forum meanwhile became a place of worship for the early Christians, who built the churches of Santi Sergius e Bacco (on the Via Sacra), of Sant'Adriano (near the Curia), and of Santi Cosma e Damiano (Temple of Peace). During the Middle Ages, it became a pasture for sheep and cattle (hence its name of "Campo Vaccino"). For many centuries the prestige of the Roman Forum was a thing of the past; not until the early 20th century was the area systematically rehabilitated with excavation campaigns that lasted for decades on end. Thanks to these efforts, much splendid evidence of the Rome of the kings as well as that of the republic and the empire has again been brought to light.

A view of the Roman Forum with Phocas' Column, the Temple of Saturn, and, on the right, a portion of the Arch of Septimius Severus.

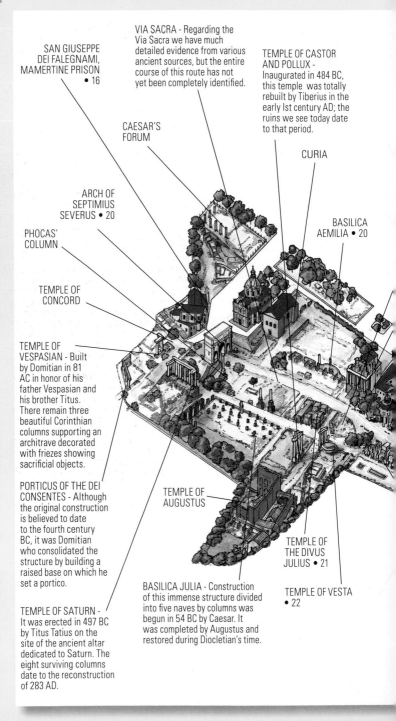

VIA SACRA - Regarding the Via Sacra we have much detailed evidence from various ancient sources, but the entire course of this route has not yet been completely identified.

SAN GIUSEPPE DEI FALEGNAMI, MAMERTINE PRISON • 16

TEMPLE OF CASTOR AND POLLUX - Inaugurated in 484 BC, this temple was totally rebuilt by Tiberius in the early Ist century AD; the ruins we see today date to that period.

CAESAR'S FORUM

CURIA

ARCH OF SEPTIMIUS SEVERUS • 20

BASILICA AEMILIA • 20

PHOCAS' COLUMN

TEMPLE OF CONCORD

TEMPLE OF VESPASIAN - Built by Domitian in 81 AC in honor of his father Vespasian and his brother Titus. There remain three beautiful Corinthian columns supporting an architrave decorated with friezes showing sacrificial objects.

PORTICUS OF THE DEI CONSENTES - Although the original construction is believed to date to the fourth century BC, it was Domitian who consolidated the structure by building a raised base on which he set a portico.

TEMPLE OF AUGUSTUS

TEMPLE OF THE DIVUS JULIUS • 21

TEMPLE OF VESTA • 22

TEMPLE OF SATURN - It was erected in 497 BC by Titus Tatius on the site of the ancient altar dedicated to Saturn. The eight surviving columns date to the reconstruction of 283 AD.

BASILICA JULIA - Construction of this immense structure divided into five naves by columns was begun in 54 BC by Caesar. It was completed by Augustus and restored during Diocletian's time.

The fulcrum of every ancient Roman city was the forum, understood as a ample public plaza: the marketplace and, in general, the city's business center, surrounded by public buildings and shops (tabernae).

REGIA - According to tradition, the Regia was originally the residence of Numa Pompilio, who took his architectural inspiration from the Etruscan models. Later it was the seat of the pontifex maximus.

TEMPLE OF ANTONINUS AND FAUSTINA • 21

TEMPLE OF THE DIVUS ROMULUS - This temple, begun by Maxentius and completed by Constantine, has remained practically intact thanks to its having been transformed, in the Middle Ages, into the atrium of the church of Santi Cosma e Damiano; the bronze door is the late Imperial Age original.

BASILICA OF MAXENTIUS • 23

SANTA FRANCESCA ROMANA

TEMPLE OF VENUS AND ROME - Hadrian built this enormous temple in 121 AD. To do so he demolished the remains of Nero's Domus Aurea and the gigantic statue of the same emperor that had given the name to the amphitheater.

ARCH OF TITUS • 24

HOUSE OF THE VESTALS - This building, traditionally attributed to Numa Pompilio, was the home of the priestesses of Vesta. It was rebuilt by Nero following the fire of 64 AD and was later restructured many times.

Every forum had a temple dedicated to the Capitoline triad (Jupiter, Minerva, and Juno); in Rome, the temple was at the top of the Campidoglio or Capitoline hill. The **temples** generally served a civic as well as religious function: Rome's Temple of Concord hosted the Senate; the Temple of Saturn, the State treasury. The **basilicas** were monumental public buildings with three or more naves, after the Greek model, that could host large meetings in covered spaces. The "forensic" basilicas were equipped with tribunes or raised platforms for the magistrates and were used for disposing of legal matters. As construction techniques were perfected, the basilica plan became more elaborate: it was enriched with lateral exedrae, and also grew in width, sporting powerful vaults like those of the Basilica of Maxentius (4th century), and developing forms that were later incorporated into Muslim and Christian sacred architecture. The *curia*, perhaps of Etruscan origin, was the building where the leaders of the community, the senators, met. Over time, the forum specialized as an urban structure: the *forum civilium*, or civic forum, was distinct from the *fora venalia*, which were dedicated exclusively to trade. In Rome, the Roman Forum and the Imperial Forums (*fora civilia*) were flanked, at the foot of the Capitol hill near the Tiber river where barges laden with goods arrived and departed, by the *Forum Holitorium*, or "legume market," the *Forum Boarium* where livestock were sold (and remains of which are still preserved), and the *Forum Piscarium*. The latter forum was moved in medieval times to a site near the Porticus of Octavia; its stalls, with inscriptions setting down the fish market regulations, still survive.

ARCH OF CONSTANTINE • 24

COLOSSEUM • 26

BASILICA AEMILIA

The basilica runs along the entire long side of the square of the Roman Forum and is the only basilica of the republican period still in existence. The basilica as a type is probably of eastern Hellenistic origin; in Rome, these buildings provided a place for carrying on the political, economic and judiciary functions of the forum when the weather made it impossible to proceed in the open air.

ARCH OF SEPTIMIUS SEVERUS

The arch is situated between the *Rostra* and the *Curia* and closes off the Roman Forum to the northeast. It was built in 203 AD to celebrate the two Parthian campaigns conducted by Septimius Severus in 195 and 197 AD. The arch is about 20 meters high, 25 meters wide and more than 11 meters deep, with three passageways, a large one in the center and two smaller ones at the sides; short flights of steps lead up to each. On top is a tall attic with a monumental inscription dedicating the arch to Septimius Severus and his son Caracalla. Representations of the monument on antique coins show that on the summit there was also once a bronze quadriga with the emperors.

On the front are four columns standing on tall plinths, dec-

The arch of Septimius Severus against the backdrop of the church of Santi Luca e Martina (left) and the Curia.

orated with reliefs of Roman soldiers and Parthian prisoners. The decoration includes two Victories above the Genii of the Seasons that frame the central opening, and personifications of the major rivers on the side openings; above, a small frieze commemorates the triumphal procession of the emperors. The keystones represent various gods: Mars appears twice in the main arch, while two female and two male figures, one of whom is Hercules, adorn the lesser arches.

But the most interesting part of the decoration is the series of four panels set above the side openings, in which the most significant episodes of the two Parthian campaigns are narrated.

TEMPLE OF ANTONINUS AND FAUSTINA

The monumental inscription on the architrave identifies this building as the temple of the emperor Antoninus Pius and his wife Faustina. It was originally erected in honor of Faustina alone, by her husband, after her death in 141 AD. When Antoninus Pius also died, in 161 AD, the temple was dedicated to the deified imperial couple by senate decree.

There are two reasons why the building has reached us in good condition; first, because the **Church of San Lorenzo in Miranda** was built inside it in the early Middle Ages, and secondly because it was unusually solidly built. Interesting fragments of sculpture, which belonged to the cult statues of the imperial couple, have been found near the temple.

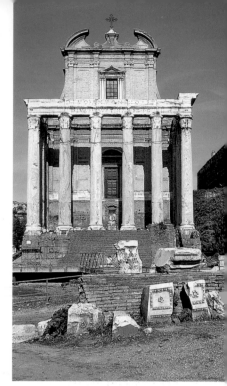

The Temple of Antoninus and Faustina, which supports the church of San Lorenzo in Miranda.

TEMPLE OF THE DIVUS JULIUS

It was built in 29 BC by Augustus, as part of his project for the restructuring of the area of the Roman Forum. The temple, dedicated to the deified Julius Caesar (the first example of such deification in Rome), stands on the site where Caesar's body was cremated before his ashes were taken to the Regia, his official residence as *pontifex maximus*. A marble column was erected here in memory of the "father of the country."

The temple may be said to reflect a true propagandistic effort by the emperor, whose aim was to have the whole forum echo with the name of the *gens Julia*.

The Vestals

As priestesses of the cult of Vesta, the vestals were the custodians of the sacred hearth and were charged with performing the various cult rites. The six vestal virgins of the only body of female priests in Rome were chosen, between the ages of six and ten, from among the daughters of the patrician families. They were required to remain in the order for thirty years and to keep a vow of chastity. Vestal virgins who broke this vow were buried alive in a subterranean chamber outside Porta Collina, in a place suitably called the "field of iniquity," while their accomplice in the transgression was condemned to death by flogging in the Comitium. But in exchange for their chastity, they enjoyed important privileges: they were subtracted from parental authority and the patria potestas passed to the pontifex maximus, they could travel in the city in a wagon (which was forbidden to ordinary women), they had reserved seats at the spectacles and ceremonies, and they were permitted to do as they best saw fit with a sort of stipend they received from the State. The order of the vestal virgins is extremely ancient and traditionally dates to the time of king Numa Pompilius.

TEMPLE OF VESTA

Located to the south of the Via Sacra in front of the Regia, this is one of the oldest temples in Rome, although its present appearance dates to 191 AD when it was restored by Julia Domna, wife of Septimius Severus. The fire sacred to Vesta, the goddess of the household hearth, had to be kept perennially burning in this temple, for disaster threatened if the flame were to go out. But this fact obviously meant that the building was frequently in danger of fire, hence the many restorations. A trapezoidal cavity in the podium, accessible only from the cella, may be the *pe-*

A view of the House of the Vestals with the church of Santa Francesca Romana in the background.

The ruins of the Basilica of Maxentius and, bottom, the remains of the Temple of Vesta.

nus Vestae; that is, the *sancta sanctorum* of the temple, a sort of storeroom that only the vestal virgins could enter that contained the objects Aeneas was said to have brought back after the destruction of Troy as proof of the universal glory of Rome. These treasures included the Palladium, an ancient wooden image of Minerva, and the images of the Penates. The *Atrium Vestae*, on the south side of the Via Sacra, was a complex consisting of the Temple of Vesta and the **House of the Vestals.**

BASILICA OF MAXENTIUS

Access to the Basilica of Maxentius, which stands outside the current archaeological area of the Roman Forum, is from the Via dei Fori Imperiali. The building was begun in 308 AD by Maxentius and completed by Constantine, who modified the internal layout by shifting the entrance from the east to the south side on the Via Sacra.

The building occupies an area of 100 by 65 meters and stands on a platform which is in part a superstructure over storerooms of considerable size. The ground plan and dimensions of the building were inspired by the majestic halls of the imperial baths, which were also called "basilicas."

ARCH OF TITUS

The Arch of Titus, the oldest of the Imperial-age arches in the Roman Forum.

The arch rises in the eastern part of the forums area, south of the Temple of Venus and Roma. As part of the medieval fortifications of the Frangipane family, it survived into the 19th century and in 1822 was restored by Valadier, as recorded in the inscription on the attic on the side facing the forum. The inscription on the side toward the Colosseum is instead coeval with the arch; it tells us that the arch was dedicated to the emperor Titus by his brother and successor Domitian to commemorate the victory of the former in the Judaic campaign of 70 AD, probably after Titus' death in 81 AD.

The Triumphal Arch

The main purpose of the triumphal arch, a creation of ancient Roman civilization, was to celebrate military might. We normally find such arches at the start of the triumphal itineraries (the "triumphs") followed by an army and its commander, or the emperor himself, as they returned victorious from a military campaign. Initially, the arches were temporary structures that were dismantled at the end of the victory celebrations, but beginning in the 1st century BC they became permanent constructions in stone, marble, or travertine, with one or three archways. Bas-relief decoration, often on virtually every surface, illustrated the salient episodes of the conflicts, heroic exploits, and the procession of military leaders, emperors, and their family members returning to the city with the victor's spoils, trophies, prisoners, and hostages. The triumphal arches were often further adorned with bronze ornaments and marble statues. In the 1st to 3rd century, arches were erected all over the Roman empire to immortalize the glorious deeds of the emperors. Triumphal arches were also erected as to celebrate civic achievements and urban improvements; this is the case, for example, of the arch erected in Benevento in honor of Trajan (2nd century).

ARCH OF CONSTANTINE

The largest of the arches erected in Rome, on the route followed by triumphal processions of antiquity between the Caelian and the Palatine hills was built in 315 AD by decree of the Senate and the Roman people to celebrate the 10th anniversary of Constantine's ascent to the throne and his victory over Maxentius in the Battle of the Milvian Bridge in 312. For decoration of the arch, a number of reliefs and sculptures from other monuments were employed. The most significant part of Constantine's decoration is the large historical frieze above the lesser openings and on the short sides of the arch. The story begins on the western side, with the *departure of Constantine from Milan*.
It continues on the south side with the representations of the *siege of Verona* by Constantine's

The majestic Arch of Constantine and, bottom, the arch against the stunning backdrop of the Colosseum.

troops and of the emperor protected by two bodyguards while a *Victory* places a wreath on his head. On the same side is a representation of the *Battle of the Milvian Bridge*, with Constantine on the bridge accompanied by the personification of *Virtus* and a *Victory*, and the *defeat of Maxentius and his troops*.

The short eastern side presents *the emperor's triumphal entrance into Rome* on a chariot preceded by Roman foot soldiers and horsemen. On the north side, *Constantine* is shown *addressing the crowd near the Rostra*: he is the only person presented frontally, in accordance with the hieratic concept of sovereignty which had by this time become well established.

A view of the exterior of the Colosseum illustrating the four-order construction plan and what remains of the travertine facing.

COLOSSEUM

The largest amphitheater ever built in Rome and the symbol par excellence of Romanism was the work of the Flavian emperors and was for this reason called the Amphiteatrum Flavium. *The name "Colosseum" was first used in the Middle Ages and derives from the colossal bronze statue of Nero as sun god which stood on the site of the vestibule of the Domus Aurea, near the amphitheater.*

Emperor Vespasian began construction of the Colosseum to provide Rome with a large permanent amphitheater in place of the Amphitheater of Taurus in the Campus Martius, a temporary wooden structure, erected by Nero after the fire of 64 AD. Work began in the early years of Vespasian's reign. After Titus had completed the fourth and fifth tiers, the amphitheater was inaugurated in 80 AD, with magnificent spectacles and games which lasted a hundred days. It assumed its present aspect and size only under Domitian. According to the sources, he added the substructures of the arena. This meant that the *naumachie* (naval battles, for which the arena had to be flooded) could no longer be held in the Colosseum as the literary sources tell us they had previously been. Additional work was carried out by Nerva, Trajan and Antoninus Pius and other emperors. The last attempt at restoration was made by Theodoric king of the Ostragoths; after his time, the building was totally abandoned. It thus became the fortress of the Frangipane family in the Middle Ages, until with the advent of further earthquakes the fallen

The Spectacles

Various types of **spectacles** were held in the Colosseum: the *munera*, or contests between gladiators, the *venationes*, or hunts of wild beasts, and the previously cited *naumachie*. Christians may or may not have been sent to their death as martyrs in the Colosseum. A final point to consider is the number of spectators the Colosseum was capable of containing: opinions vary, but the figure must have been around 50,000.

Access to seats in the cavea was based on social class: the higher up the seat, the less influential its occupant. The inscriptions still readable on some of the extant tiers inform us that they were reserved for specific categories of citizens. The emperor's box was at the south end of the minor axis, where the consuls and Vestal Virgins also sat. The box at the north extremity was for the prefect of the city (*praefectus urbis*) and other magistrates.

material began to be removed for use in new constructions. From the 15th through the mid-18th century, the once-great amphitheater was transformed into a simple quarry for blocks of travertine until it was consecrated by Pope Benedict XV.

Views of the cavea and the arena, with the visitors' itinerary.

The amphitheater was inaugurated in 80 AD with spectacles and games that lasted, according to sources of the time, one hundred days, during which thousands of wild animals and many gladiators were killed in combat.

The Construction of the Colosseum

The building is **elliptical in form** and measures 188 x 156 meters at the perimeter and 86 x 54 meters inside; it is almost 49 meters in height. The **four-story** facade is built entirely of **travertine**. The three lower stories have 80 arches each, supported by piers and framed by encased three-quarter columns that are Doric on the first level, Ionic on the second, and Corinthian on the third. The three lower levels are crowned by a fourth-story attic, on the exterior of which, in the walls between one Corinthian parastade and the next, there alternate square windows and blank spaces where the gilded shields once hung. The beams that supported the large canopy (velarium) that protected the spectators from the sun were fitted into a row of holes in the upper cornice. The arches of the ground floor level were numbered to indicate the entrance to the various tiers of seats in the cavea. The **four entrances of honor**, reserved for upper class persons of rank such as magistrates, members of the religious colleges, and the Vestal Virgins, were situated at the ends of the principal axes of the building and were unnumbered. The entrance on the north side was preceded by a small two-columned portico opening on a corridor, decorated with stuccowork, that led to the imperial tribune. The external arcades led to a twin set of circular corridors from which stairs led

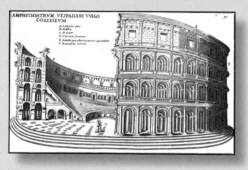

to the aisles (vomitoria) of the cavea; the second floor had a similar double ambulacrum, and so did the third, but with a lower ceiling than the other two, while at the attic level two single corridors ran one over the other.

Inside, the **cavea** was separated from the arena by a podium almost four meters high, behind which the seats of honor were arranged. The cavea was divided in the horizontal sense into three orders (*maeniana*) separated by walls in masonry (*baltei*). The first two maeniana (the second was subdivided once more into upper and lower sections) had marble seats and were cut through vertically by the entrance aisles (*vomitoria*) and stairs. The result was to create sectors called cunei; it was therefore possible to assign seat numbers by tier, cuneus and single seat. The third *maenianum*, or *maenianum summum*, had wooden tiers and was separated from the *maenianum secundum* below by a high wall. There was a colonnade with a gallery reserved for the women, above which a terrace provided standing room only for the lower classes. The tiers closest to the arena were reserved for senators.

The **arena** was originally covered with wooden floorboards which could be removed as required. In the case of hunts of ferocious animals, the spectators in the cavea were protected by a metal grating topped by elephant tusks and rotating cylinders placed horizontally in such a manner as to make it impossible for the wild animals to claw their way up. The **area below the arena floor** contained all the structures necessary for the presentation of the spectacles: cages for the animals, settings and illusionistic devices, storerooms for the gladiators' weapons, machines, etc.

Villa Borghese: a mosaic with scenes of gladiators (3rd-4th cent.)from the Torrenuova estate in the Tusculum area.

The Gladiators

The story of the gladiators is a long one that goes back in time to the Etruscan world, where they were key players in funerary rites celebrated to drive off the spirits of the dead. What began as human sacrifice soon turned into combat between prisoners of war, slaves, prisoners sentenced to death, and later even free citizens who sought to capture a moment of glory and celebrity. The phenomenon reached its highest peaks of splendor and greatest diffusion in the Roman world, where the gladiatorial combats were enormously popular—as we see from the huge arenas consecrated to them. And despite the ban imposed by Emperor Constantine in 325 AD, gladiatorial games continued until the year 404. There were about 20 types of gladiators, classified according to the arms and armor each used in combat. The combat, which was announced by special edicta, lasted an entire day and attracted thousands of spectators. And it was the crowd, these impassioned spectators, who decreed the survival or death of the gladiator defeated after a ferocious, no-holds-barred match: a mass waving of handkerchiefs spared him, especially if he had fought valiantly and intrepidly; otherwise, by turning their thumbs down, the spectators voted for his execution. The crowd's sentence was final: even the emperor, when he attended the games, turned to the crowd to hear their judgment before sparing the gladiator or decreeing his death. But if all went well, the victor was regaled with crowns of laurel, money, honor, and immense glory. The memory of the gladiators lives on in the funerary monuments erected in their honor, with inscriptions that have transmitted the moving, proud eulogies of wives, children, concubines, and even trainers.

Facing page, top: Museo Nazionale Romano, the *Chariot Race*, a floor mosaic lifted from the Villa di Baccano.

Right and on the facing page, the arena and the exterior of the Colosseum in two 17th-century engravings.

PALATINE HILL

This is the most famous of Rome's hills and it retains the earliest memories of the old city. In fact, it was on the Palatine that the first groups of huts were built, way before the city spread to encompass the adjacent hills. Prominent public buildings, large temples and many private dwellings such as those of Cicero, Crassus and Tiberius Gracchus stood here.

Later on, the hill became the residence of the emperors of Rome and the site of their sumptuous palaces, including the **Domus Augustana**, the **Domus Flavia**, the **Domus Transitoria**, the **Domus Aurea**, and the **Domus Tiberiana**, of which considerable remains are still extant. Later still, the Palatine was the residence of the Gothic kings and of many popes and emperors of the Western Empire; in the Middle Ages convents and churches were built. Finally, in the 16th century, most of the hill

HUTS OF ROMULUS - Some very ancient evidence of constructions from the prehistorical and the early Iron Age, the oldest in the architectural history of Rome; traditionally, the **home of the founder of the city.**

DOMUS TIBERIANA - The house of Tiberius was the first of the imperial palaces to be conceived organically as such, and the first to be built on the Palatine. Only a small part of the building complex has been excavated, since the area it occupied became the Horti Farnesiani in the 16th century.

HOUSE OF LIVIA - The house of Augustus' wife Livia, in which the Emperor himself probably also lived, is one of the most precious examples of early imperial Roman architecture.

DOMUS FLAVIA • 34

DOMUS AUGUSTANA • 33

CIRCUS MAXIMUS • 35

PALATINE STADIUM

A view of the ruins of the Domus Augustana.

was occupied by the immense structures of **Villa Farnese** and the **Horti Farnesiani** (the first real botanical gardens). Archaeological excavations begun on the Palatine in the 18th century brought to light much evidence of Rome's past, including the remains of the Domus Augustana, splendid paintings of republican period, and the remains of the first dwellings that stood on the hill, not to mention the magnificent 16th-century entrance portal to the Horti Farnesiani.

DOMUS AUGUSTANA

The building of Domitian's grandiose palace on the Palatine gave the hill its definitive topographical disposition and firmly established its role as the site of the imperial residences. The building was begun in the early years of Domitian's reign and in the main completed by 92 AD, although some parts, such as the stadium, were finished later. It was used as the emperor's palace until the end of the

Empire. The complex is divided into three parts: the *Domus Flavia,* which was used for state functions, the *Domus Augustana* proper, a private wing, and finally the *Stadium,* or large garden in the shape of a circus.

The Domus Augustana represents an important moment in Roman architecture. Here, Domitian's architect Rabirius created what was to become the canonic formula for the dynastic residence: a synthesis of structural functionality - with the division into official and private sectors - and extravagant decoration, in which the blend of curved and straight lines in the ground plan and the illusionistic and perspective effects, already present in Nero's Domus Aurea and here reproposed, were made a near science.

DOMUS FLAVIA

This construction consisted of three aisles separated by columns and terminating in an apse. At the center of the structure are the remains of the Aula Regia, or throne room, in which the emperor held audience. Significant parts of another room, the **lararium**, or the emperor's private chapel, are also still extant.

Facing page, from top to bottom: the Horti Farnesiani, the ruins of the Domus Augustana, the ruins of the Domus Severiana seen from the Circus Maximus, and the remains of the octagonal fountain in the Domus Flavia.

The vast arena of the Circus Maximus as it appears today.

Museo della Civiltà Romana: detail of a bas-relief from the first century AD of the races at the Circus Maximus.

The Circus Maximus in a 17th-century reconstruction.

The Circus Maximus

Although the Circus Maximus, the first construction of its kind in Rome, was initially built of wood, the sections in masonry gradually increased in number, beginning with the **carceres**, a sort of starting-gate for the horses. The circus consisted of a long track surrounded by a **cavea** with various tiers of seats, broken, on the side adjacent to the Palatine, by the **pulvinar**, a building with a tribune on which were placed the statues of the divinities that presided over the spectacles and from which the emperor watched the contests. The Circus measured 600 x 200 meters and had a capacity of 320,000 spectators. The most important of the events held there were the chariot races during the first week of September on occasion of the Ludi Romani, games which opened with a religious procession in which the highest religious and civil authorities of the city took part. Today, only the lay of the land, much higher than the first arena, betrays the form of the original structure.

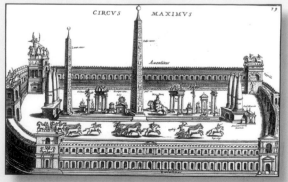

IMPERIAL FORUMS

The Imperial Forums were built near the earlier forum of republican times and were created with the scope of enhancing the prestige of the city and providing the citizens with a place for their markets and one where they could listen to the harangues and participate in religious ceremonies.: During the Middle Ages, a minimal portion was recovered and a small residential district came into being among the Roman ruins. Most of the area, however, was invaded by water and became a mud-field, called at the time the Pantani ("bogs"): the splendid buildings of Imperial times were destroyed or gravely damaged. Forgotten for centuries, the area was partially urbanized in the Renaissance, but not until the 19th and above all the 20th centuries were the remains of this once magnificent architecture brought to light and the Via dei Fori Imperiali created.

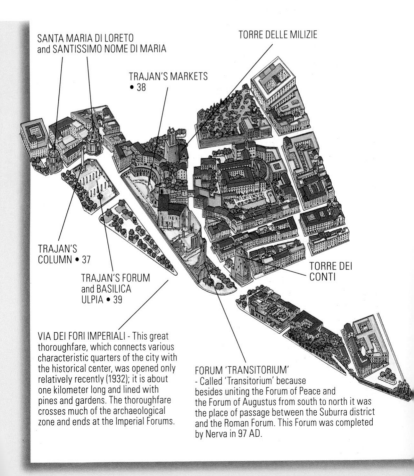

SANTA MARIA DI LORETO and SANTISSIMO NOME DI MARIA

TORRE DELLE MILIZIE

TRAJAN'S MARKETS
• 38

TRAJAN'S COLUMN • 37

TRAJAN'S FORUM and BASILICA ULPIA • 39

TORRE DEI CONTI

VIA DEI FORI IMPERIALI - This great thoroughfare, which connects various characteristic quarters of the city with the historical center, was opened only relatively recently (1932); it is about one kilometer long and lined with pines and gardens. The thoroughfare crosses much of the archaeological zone and ends at the Imperial Forums.

FORUM 'TRANSITORIUM' - Called 'Transitorium' because besides uniting the Forum of Peace and the Forum of Augustus from south to north it was the place of passage between the Suburra district and the Roman Forum. This Forum was completed by Nerva in 97 AD.

TRAJAN'S COLUMN

The column that stands in Trajan's Forum was dedicated in 113 AD. The Doric *centenaria* (that is, 100 Roman feet or 39.77 meters tall) column is composed of 18 drums of Luna marble. It stands on a high cubic base with four eagles holding garlands at the corners and low relief trophies of stacks of Dacian weapons on three sides. All together, it is almost 40 meters high; the statue of Trajan that once topped it was lost; in 1587 Pope Sixtus V set one of *Saint Peter* in its place. The entrance door to the monument is on its main side facing the Basilica Ulpia. Set above it is a panel supported by two Victories, with an inscription celebrating the donation of the column to the emperor by the Senate and the Roman people as an indication of the height of the hill before it was leveled to make way for the new forum. Actually, the column was meant to serve as the tomb of the emperor: the entrance in the base leads, on the left, to an antechamber and then a large room where a golden urn containing Trajan's ashes was kept. From the same entrance, but to the right, is a spiral staircase of 185 steps, cut in the marble, that leads to the top of the column. A continuous frieze, about 200 meters long and varying in height from 90 to 125 centimeters, moves around the shaft of the column like an unrolled *volumen* to represent Trajan's two victorious Dacian campaigns of 101-102

Trajan's Column, etched with the spiral frieze narrating the exploits of emperor.

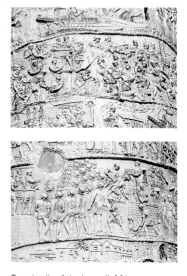

Two details of the bas-relief frieze
on Trajan's Column.

and 105-106 AD. The two narrations are separated by a figure of Victory writing on a shield. All the phases of the two wars are minutely described with precise geographical and topographical details. Battle scenes alternate with representations of troop movements, the construction of encampments, bridges, and roads, speeches made to the troops, sieges, the deportation of the conquered enemy, etc. The documentary and didactic purpose is evident from the inclusion of detailed items of information meant to help the spectator understand the events more clearly. There are more than 2500 figures in the frieze and Trajan appears about 60 times. The relief was originally painted, but the chromatic decoration has survived only in few places. There may also have been painted inscriptions with the names of the places where the action took place. The work is attributed to the so-called "Master of the Feats of Trajan," who may perhaps be identified with Apollodorus of Damascus, the architect of Trajan's Forum.

TRAJAN'S MARKETS

The construction of Trajan's Forum required the removal of part of the Quirinal hill; the architect,

The hemicycle of Trajan's Markets.

The Promenade through Trajan's Markets

The promenade, that can be reached from Via IV Novembre and the Salita del Grillo, runs through the several levels of the markets and offers a fine view of the Imperial Forums.

From Via Biberatica we can take the promenade as far as the small "small hemicycle", and from here we continue to a panoramic terrace and then the green, shaded garden of the Torre delle Milizie.

A view of the visitors' itinerary through Trajan's Markets.

Apollodorus of Damascus (who also built Trajan's Forum), made brilliant use of the cutaway face to realize a unified structural complex which we call Trajan's Markets. Trajan's Markets probably functioned as a sort of wholesale outlet for staple foodstuffs such as grain, oil and wine, managed by the state through imperial personnel who supplied the *negotiatores* of the provinces. Retail sales were probably also conducted at "political" prices inferior to going market prices - and it was probably here that on occasion the emperor distributed foodstuffs to the people (the so-called *congiaria*).

The Loggia of the Knights of Rhodes seen from the colonnade of Trajan's Forum.

TRAJAN'S FORUM AND BASILICA ULPIA

This was the most important public work carried out by Trajan and his architect Apollodorus of Damascus, and involved elimination of the ridge between the Capitoline and the Quirinal hills. The impressive complex was built between 106 and 113 AD and was financed by the proceeds of the Dacian war that had just been concluded. The Basilica Ulpia is the largest basilica ever built in Rome. It is 170 meters long and almost 60 meters wide, and takes its name from the family name of the emperor.

FONTANA DI TREVI

This may not be the most beautiful fountain in Rome, but it is without doubt the most famous. Both Pietro da Cortona and above all Bernini, who began the undertaking, had a hand in the project. The death of Pope Urban VIII brought work to a standstill and it was not until about a hundred years later that Clement XII entrusted the work to Nicola Salvi, who finished the fountain between 1732 and 1751.

The design of the fountain is highly symbolic, with various intellectual connotations. A tall and sober **Arch of Triumph** (the Palace of Neptune) dominates the scene from on high, with a row of four Corinthian columns surmounted by an attic with statues and a balustrade. A large niche at the center of the arch lends balance and symmetry to the whole ensemble. A smaller niche to the left contains the statue of *Abundance* by F. Valle, above which is a relief by Andrea Bergondi depicting *Agrippa Approving the Plans for the Aqueduct*.

The niche on the right contains

The jutting mass of the Fontana di Trevi; top, the statue of Neptune, god of the seas.

Another view of the fountain and a detail of a triton.

the figure of *Salubrity*, also by F. Valle, surmounted by a relief of the *Virgin Showing the Soldiers the Way*, by G. B. Grossi.

The central niche seems to impart movement to the commanding figure of Neptune, who with a firm hand guides a chariot drawn by two sea horses, known as the "spirited horse" and the "placid horse," names obviously derived from the way in which the two animals have been represented.

As they gallop over the water, the horses are guided in their course by the figures of Tritons emerging from the water sculpted by P. Bracci in 1762. The setting all around consists of rocks.

PIAZZA DI SPAGNA AND TRINITÀ DEI MONTI

One of the most characteristic of Roman squares, Piazza di Spagna runs for 270 meters and is divided into two triangular areas. The square takes its name from the **Palazzo di Spagna**, seat since the 17th century of the Spanish ambassador to the Holy See. It is famous for its magnificent buildings, elegant shops, and for the illustrious personages who sojourned here in the past: from the enigmatic Cagliostro, who held his masonic meetings tinged with magic in an inn, to Casanova, who mentioned the square in his famous *Memoirs*, to Keats, who lived and died at No. 26, now a small **museum** dedicated to

Left, a detail of the Sallustian obelisk.
The monumental stairs leading up to the church of Trinità dei Monti.

the great poet. Other notable buildings, such as the **Palazzo di Propaganda Fide** with the conjoined **Church of the Re Magi**, and the aforementioned complex of the Palazzo di Spagna, also overlook the square.

At the center of the square is the **Fontana della Barcaccia**, set against the theatrical backdrop of the famous *Scalinata di Trinità dei Monti* (or the Spanish Steps), which leads to the equally famous Piazza di Trinità dei Monti with the **Sallustian obelisk**, formerly in the Horti Sallustiani, at its center. This square is dominated by the bulk of the **Church of Trinità dei Monti.**

SPANISH STEPS OR SCALINATA DI TRINITÀ DEI MONTI

The theatrical effect of these famous steps and their powerful evocative quality is part of the history of the image of the city. Built entirely in travertine by Francesco De Sanctis between 1723 and 1726, the Scalinata consists of twelve flights which widen and narrow in compact but varied stages in no way bound by rigid schemes, in line with rococo architectural concepts. The steps begin in Piazza di Spagna and rise to Piazza di Trinità dei Monti.

Fontana della Barcaccia

Perhaps the most congenial work by Pietro Bernini, father of the more famous Gian Lorenzo, this fountain (1627-29) stands at the center of the Piazza di Spagna and acts as a sort of fulcrum for the many buildings all around. It is a lively and brilliantly-conceived representation of a sinking boat leaking water at the stern and prow. The idea seems to have come from Pope Urban VII, who was struck by the sight of a boat that had sunk when the Tiber flooded.

A side ramp of the Trinità dei Monti stairs (Spanish Steps).

The Fontana della Barcaccia at the foot of the Spanish Steps.

CHURCH OF TRINITÀ DEI MONTI

One of the most impressive of the Franciscan churches in the city, Trinità dei Monti was begun in 1503 by Louis XII, but has been remodeled over the course of time. The sober **facade**, by Carlo Maderno, with a single order of pilasters and a wide columned portal, is surmounted by an attic with a large balustrade and is preceded by a **staircase** designed by Domenico Fontana (1587).

Church of Trinità dei Monti: the single broad nave is home to precious works of art.

VIA CONDOTTI

Caffè Greco

This famous café, frequented by artists and literati such as De Chirico, Mafai and Scipione, still preserves its original paintings and furnishings. It is located in Via Condotti, one of the city's most fashionable streets with its numerous shops and cafés.

PIAZZA DI SPAGNA

Babington's Tea Room

More than one hundred years ago, in 1893, when tea was still sold in pharmacies in Italy, two enterprising women English women, Anna Maria Babington and Isabel Cargill, journeyed from England to Rome and opened this unique establishment. Since then, the tea room and shop has perpetuated an exquisitely English taste and atmosphere at the original premises in Piazza di Spagna, offering rare blends of tea and delicious breakfast, lunch, and snack specialties.

A view, from the Pincian Hill, of Piazza del Popolo and the Flaminian obelisk.

PIAZZA DEL POPOLO

Piazza del Popolo, one of the most characteristic areas of Neoclassical Rome, is the child of Giuseppe Valadier's creative genius in the field of town planning and architecture. The original design dates to 1793. Distinctive features of the square are the low exedrae defining its sides, topped by statues of the *Four Seasons*, and the two centrally-placed fountains, *Neptune and the Tritons* and *Rome between the Tiber and the Aniene Rivers*, that set off the obelisk. All the sculpture dates to the first half of the 19th century and is the work of Gnaccarini, Laboureur, Stocchi, Baini, and Ceccarini.

Goethe Museum
The Goethe Museum, in Via del Corso 17, occupies the rooms where the author of *Italian Journey* lived during his stay in Rome from 1786 to 1788. The museum preserves portraits of J. Wolfgang von Goethe (one by Andy Warhol!), drawings by J. H. W. Tischbein, a close friend of the author, works by Goethe, and many other books on the history of cultural relations between Germany and Italy.

Flaminian Obelisk

The obelisk that since 1589 has stood in the center of Piazza del Popolo is an exceptional legacy of classical Rome. Dating to 1200 BC, it was originally erected by the Egyptian pharaoh Rameses II in Heliopolis, opposite the Temple of the Sun. Augustus brought it to Rome and re-erected it in the Circus Maximus. Under Pope Sixtus V it was moved to its present site, and under Leo XII (early 19th century) it became the centerpiece of Valadier's fountains with their four basins and marble lions.

ARA PACIS AUGUSTAE

The altar was begun on 4 July in 13 BC, near the Via Flaminia on property belonging to Agrippa. The *dedicatio* (that is, the inauguration ceremony upon completion of the work) was held on 30 January in 9 BC. The discovery of the Ara Pacis dates to 1568, when nine of its sculpted blocks were found during construction of the Renaissance Palazzo Fiano (now Palazzo Almagià). In 1870, Von Duhn identified these marble fragments for the first time as remains of the famous monument. Systematic excavations begun in 1903 brought to light the supporting structures of the altar; the excavations were finally terminated, in 1937-38, on occasion of the Augustan bimillenial celebrations, and the altar was reconstructed in a pavilion built for this purpose next to the Mausoleum of Augustus, near the Tiber. At present, therefore, the Ara Pacis no longer occupies its original site and its orientation has also been changed, from east-west to north-south. The monument is composed of a rectangular marble enclosure on a podium. It was originally accessed via a staircase, with two large doors that opened on the long. The altar itself, set on a three-stepped podium, is inside the enclosure; on the west, five other steps permitted the priest to reach the top of the altar on which the sacrificial rites took place. The entire enclosure is covered with rich sculptural decoration both inside and out.

Travertine, plaster, glass and steel are the materials that enclose the Ara Pacis in a **protective shell** creating a museum and defending it against damage from smog. Natural light that streams in from the skylights combines with and enhances the artificial light to reveal the beautiful translucence and shadings of the marble altar.

The Ara Pacis and the elegant protective structure designed by architect Richard Meier.

A view of the Mausoleum of Augustus.

MAUSOLEUM OF AUGUSTUS

The dynastic tomb of the first emperor of Rome is a circular structure consisting of a series of concentric walls in tufa connected by walls radiating out from the center. The first accessible chamber lies at the end of the long entrance corridor (*dromos*) which cuts through the structures described above. Two entrances in this wall lead to the annular corridor which rings the circular cella. The tomb of Augustus was here, in correspondence to the bronze statue of the emperor that stood at the top of the pier.

ELEPHANT OF PIAZZA DELLA MINERVA

Considered one of Bernini's most delightful inventions, the elephant serves as the support for the Egyptian **obelisk** dating to the 6th century BC. Sculpted by Ercole Ferrata in 1667, it is so small in relation to the column that it is popularly known as "Minerva's chick," even though the inscription on the base makes of it the symbol of a robust intellect capable of supporting great wisdom, the role assigned to the towering obelisk above.

Caffè Giolitti®

Just a few steps from the Pantheon and from Montecitorio is one of Rome's best-known ice-cream parlors, Giolitti. Its origins can be traced back to 1890, when it was a simple dairy shop on the Salita del Grillo. Having become purveyors to the royal family thanks to the quality of their products, the Giolitti family opened other shops and began producing an ice-cream that soon became fabulously famous in the capital and beyond.
Today, the Giolitti ice-cream parlor is a historic meeting-place for Romans, Italy's political class, and a "must" on the sightseeing itinerary of any foreign tourist.

The elephant, designed by Bernini, that supports the 6th-century BC Egyptian obelisk in Piazza della Minerva. The inscription on the base reads in part: *robustae mentis esse solidam sapientiam sustinere* meaning ". . . a strong mind is needed to hold great wisdom."

Pantheon: the inscription above the pronaos attests to the building's patrimony:
"Marcus Agrippa, son of Lucius, consul for the third time, made it."

PANTHEON

*In the pagan religions, the "pantheon" was the temple dedicated
to "all the gods." Over time, the term has come to stand for
a mausoleum of illustrious figures. The Panthéon of Paris, for
example, in neoclassical style, preserves the remains of such
famous men in French history and culture as Jean Jacques
Rousseau and Voltaire, Jean Jaurès, and Jean-Paul Marat. Rome's
first Pantheon was built under Emperor Augustus in honor of his
family's protector gods; after the fire of 80 AD, it was rebuilt and
modified under Hadrian, who is responsible for its current aspect.
The Pantheon is one of the most extraordinary of ancient Roman
monuments in virtue of its excellent state of preservation, its
unequalled grandeur, and its architectural plan, which has been
copied time and time again in neoclassical buildings in all parts of
the world. Raphael (Raffaello Sanzio) and members of the House
of Savoy, Italy's last reigning family, are interred here.*

Of all the buildings of ancient Rome, the Pantheon is the best preserved, thanks to its having been donated to Pope Boniface IV by the Byzantine emperor Phocas and later transformed into a church with the name of Santa Maria ad Martyres (609 AD). The first building was erected in 27 BC by Marcus Vipsanius Agrippa, Augustus' faithful advisor, as part of the general urban improvement work targeting the central area of the Campus Martius, which had just then become his property. The temple was conceived for the glorification of the *gens Julia* and was called the

Traditionally, on Pentecost Sunday, or "Pasqua delle Rose," during the high mass celebrated by the pope, thousands of rose petals, symbol of the Holy Spirit, are showered through the oculus onto the assembled worshippers.

Pantheon (*sanctissimum*): all the planetary divinities in addition to Mars and Venus, the protectors of Augustus' family, may have been honored here. Agrippa's building, as excavations carried out in the late 19th century have shown, was rectangular and faced south, not north as now. The facade was on the long side; it was preceded by a pronaos, in front of which was an open circular area paved in travertine. The temple was damaged in the fire of 80 AD and was restored by Domitian. It was again damaged by fire in Trajan's time, and was completely rebuilt by Hadrian between 118 and 128 AD in the form we still see today. The facade of the large columned **porch** is still composed of eight columns in grey granite. Behind the porch is a massive construction in brick, which joins the porch and the

Raffaello Sanzio
(Urbino 1483 - Rome 1520)

Raphael, son of a court painter to the Duke of Urbino, was born in Italy's Marche region in 1483, at the height of the Renaissance, a year after his future master, Pietro Perugino, painted the wall fresco of the *Christ Giving the Keys to Saint Peter* for the Sistine Chapel. In 1500, the year Michelangelo produced his *Pietà* for Saint Peter's, Raphael debuted as a painter. In 1504, he moved to Florence, the nerve center of that lively artistic climate that had surrounded him since his birth.

In the Tuscan city, dominated by the figures of Leonardo and Michelangelo, Raphael developed his personal style and perfected his flair for refined portraiture, which emerges with extreme grace in his many representations of the Virgin, and for balanced composition of his pictorial spaces. One especially significant work dating to this period is the famous *Madonna of the Goldfinch* (1504). Raphael was invited to Rome, and the Vatican, in 1508 by Pope Julius II; here, he created the frescoes in what are now known as the Raphael Rooms of the Vatican; they are the highest expression of his manner of depicting sacred subjects, which melds humanization of the characters with idealization of the spaces and which created an iconography that has remained unchanged down through our times. As chief architect of the Fabbrica di San Pietro, he commissioned Michelangelo and Giuliano da San Gallo to design and build the new Saint Peter's Basilica. In accordance with the artist's wishes, Raphael was interred in the Pantheon, a fitting resting place for a "Roman" artist whose unique artistic legacy centers on the city.

The interior of the Pantheon. Bottom, the tomb of Raphael.

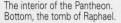

rotunda, a gigantic cylinder with a wall that is six meters thick and divided into three superposed sectors marked externally by cornices. The wall lightens as it rises, and moreover is not always solid, being cut through by brick vaulting in various places. The height of the rotunda at the top of the dome is precisely that of its diameter (43.30 meters): the interior space is thus a perfect sphere. The **dome** is a masterpiece of engineering: it is the widest masonry dome ever raised and was cast in a single operation over an enormous wooden framework. The **interior** of the building has six distyle niches at the sides and a semicircular exedra at the back; in between are eight small aediculae with alternating arched and triangular pediments. The dome is decorated with five tiers of hollow coffers that cover it completely except for a smooth band near the *oculus*, the circular opening (9 meters in diameter) that provides the only light to the interior.

Caravaggio in Rome

Just a few steps from Piazza Navona is a precious group of masterpieces by Michelangelo Merisi, better known as Caravaggio (Milano 1571- Porto Ercole 1610).

The Contarelli Chapel in the church of **San Luigi dei Francesi** is the home of three important canvases, all dedicated to the figure of Saint Matthew, that trace artist's personal style as it matured. Here, in fact, are the *Vocation of Saint Matthew* and the *Martyrdom of Saint Matthew*, at the sides, painted between 1599 and July of 1600,

Church of San Luigi dei Francesi: Caravaggio, the *Vocation*.

and *Saint Matthew and the Angel* (1602) on the altar. In the nearby church of **Sant'Agostino**, the altar of the first chapel on the left is graced by the *Madonna of the Pilgrims*, dated 1603 – 1606, with its crudely veristic tones. Two famous Caravaggios, the *Conversion of Saint* Paul and the *Crucifixion of Saint Peter* (1600-1601), are on display in the Cerasi Chapel in **Santa Maria del Popolo**, in Piazza del Popolo. Considered one of the foremost exponents of the Baroque school of painting, Caravaggio was born in Milan and trained in the Lombard realist school. At twenty, he came to Rome, to the workshop of the Cavalier d'Arpino, and in just a few years, in the era of such masters as Rubens, Annibale Carracci, and Guido Reni, established his reputation among the great patrons of art. Outlawed and condemned to death for having mortally wounded a dueling adversary, Caravaggio fled Rome in 1606, but not before having created a legacy of notable works that are now on exhibit in the city's churches and its many museums.

Church of San Luigi dei Francesi: Caravaggio, the *Martyrdom* (bottom) of Saint Matthew.

The Fontana dei Quattro Fiumi, at the center of Piazza Navona, and two details.

PIAZZA NAVONA

This square, the most famous of Baroque Rome, covers the site of Domitian's stadium. The name would seem to derive from a popular corruption of the term for the competitive (*in agone*) games that were held here in Roman times. From Domitian onward, the stadium was used almost exclusively for sports events, including the

The church of Sant'Agnese in Agone from the Fontana del Moro or Fountain of the Moor.

famous regatta held in August, in which the participants wore the colors of the nobles and the civic clergy. Today, the square hosts the Christmas market of the Befana from mid-December to Twelfth Night. But the real attraction is Gian Lorenzo Bernini's famous **Fontana dei Fiumi** (Fountain of the Four Rivers - 1651), which won for the artist the admiration and protection of the then-pope Innocent X. The rivers represented in the fountain are the *Danube*, the *Ganges*, the *Nile*, and the *Rio de la Plata*. They are arranged on a steep rocky crag from which a Roman obelisk, taken from the Circus of Maxentius, rises daringly into the air.

Aligned with the Fountain of the Four Rivers are the **Fountain of the Moor**, at the south end in front of the **Palazzo Pamphili**, and the **Fountain of Neptune**, formerly "of the Calderari," at the northern end of the square.

Bas-relief of the *Funerary Banquet*

The *Ludovisi Throne*

PALAZZO ALTEMPS

The historic Palazzo Altemps, the original architecture and decoration of which have now been recovered thanks to painstaking restoration, is home to the History of Collecting section of the National Museum of Rome (Museo Nazionale Romano). Outstanding among the holdings of Palazzo Altemps, an extraordinary gallery of Roman and Greek statuary, are the Altemps, Boncompagni-Ludovisi, and Mattei collections, and the museum's Egyptian collection. The oldest is the **Altemps Collection**, named for a great collector of ancient art, Austrian Cardinal Marco Sittico Altemps, The **Boncompagni Ludovisi Collection**, the largest and the most prestigious, was begun by Cardinal Ludovico Ludovisi who collected examples of ancient statuary to adorn his villa built around 1621

between the Pincio and the Quirinale on the site of the ancient *Horti Sallustiani*. Other statues came to light during the work for construction of the villa; the collection thus acquired the so-called *Acrolito* and the *Galatian Killing his Wife* (found together with the *Dying Galatian*, which is now in the Musei Capitolini) and later there were added the *Ares*, the *Athena*, and the *Large Ludovisi Sarcophagus*. The **Museo Nazionale Romano**, a precious archaeological institution founded in the late 1800s, also maintains branches in two other locations: the complex of the Baths of Diocletian, where we find an important nucleus of statuary in the *Octagonal Hall*, and Palazzo Massimo, divided into sections illustrating the evolution of Roman art from the Republican era through Imperial times.

CHURCH OF SANT'AGNESE IN AGONE

The church dates to the second half of the 17th century. It was begun by Carlo Rainaldi and finished by Borromini, who followed the original plans except for the imaginative concave. The seven altars along the round perimeter of the Greek-cross interior of the building are decorated with magnificent marble statues.

Palazzo Spada, the columned "perspective gallery" by Borromini.

On the facing page, from Palazzo Altemps: center, *Hermes Loghios*; bottom, the exhibition hall with *Herakles* (left).

Pasquino

One of the famous 'talking statues' to which the Roman people traditionally posted brief satyric verses ridiculing those in power, called *pasquinades*. The statue is actually one figure from a Roman sculptural group of *Menelaus Supporting Patrocles*, found in 1501 and installed in its present location by order of Cardinal Oliviero Carafa.

PALAZZO AND GALLERIA SPADA

This palace, today the home of the Council of State, surprises the visitor, with its architectural affiatus and the imaginative design of the decoration. Borromini made a number of fantastic modifications to the original structure: the most sensational was to create the so-called **Galleria Prospettica**, a corridor nine meters in length that thanks to peculiar architectural sleights of hand appears instead to be 37 meters long. The Galleria Spada, which contains the works of art collected by Cardinal Bernardino Spada, is instead of a completely different nature. Here, works by the most important painters of the seventeenth century are exhibited in accordance with the tried-and-true criterion of the seventeenth-century private picture gallery: Titian, Mattia Preti, Baciccia, Guercino, Guido Reni, Annibale Caracci, Rubens, Solimena, and Orazio and Artemisia Gentileschi are only a few of the artists represented here.

CAMPO DE' FIORI R.VI

Campo dei Fiori in the
1700s, in a period print.

The monument to
Giordano Bruno, erected
in the late 19th century.

The special atmosphere that makes Campo de' Fiori
one of Rome's most authentic milieus changes hour
by hour, just as its colors and the sounds that invade
the fascinating space, bounded by picturesque small
buildings and charming shops, make spectrum shifts
according to the time of day. In the morning, the
brightly-colored **market** fills the square with the
voices of the hawkers who sing the praises of their
wares: fruit and vegetables, meats and cheeses,
clothing and household goods. But in the late morning, as the last of the vendors' stalls are carted
away, silence falls as though by magic and the feel
of Campo de' Fiori becomes almost intimate, with
the only sounds the discreet footfalls of Roman and
foreign passers-by. At dusk, especially in summer,
the square comes alive again, with visitors attracted
by the **typical cafes**, **taverns**, **restaurants**, and **wine-
shops** that face on it and the streets off it, while stroll-
ing musicians fill the air with their music.
In the past, however, the spectacles and pastimes
were of quite a different kind: although Campo de'

On these pages, images suggesting the typical atmosphere of the district. Bottom left, Piazza Farnese.

Fiori was the theater of festive events such as horse-races, jousts, and tournaments, it was also the site of executions, including that of the philosopher **Giordano Bruno**, who was accused of heresy and burned at the stake in February of the year 1600, as the 19th-century monument by Ettore Ferrari, at the center of the square, reminds us. And it was so even despite its poetical name, which traditionally derives from the flowers that grew on the site when it was no more than a meadow sloping down toward the Tiber - that is, before Pope Eugenius IV had it paved in the mid-1400s. Another tradition has the name deriving from Flora, the mistress of that Pompey who built his grandiose theater, adjoining the Temple of Venus Victrix, on the site that is now the square.

Over the centuries homes and palaces, but also hotels, inns, and taverns, were built lining the square: for example, the Hostaria della Vacca and that 'della Fontana', both managed by Vanozza Cattanei, the mistress of Pope Alexander VI Borgia. They are still recognizable thanks to the signs that attracted customers, the forerunners of the picturesque stopping-places that still today offer hospitality to both the Roman and the tourist to the city.

The propylaea of the
Porticus of Octavia.

Bottom, an ancient marble
market stall from the era
in which the Porticus
of Octavia was the site
of the fish market.

PORTICUS OF OCTAVIA

The complex, built by Augustus between 33 and 23 BC and dedicated to his sister Octavia, was destroyed by the fire of 80 AD and restored by Domitian. A second reconstruction was undertaken by Septimius Severus after another fire in 191 AD. The remains we see today are those of the latter version. The parts of the complex that are still visible and in good condition include the propylaea on the south side, which projected inwards and outwards with two

Palazzo Orsini, incorporated into the remains of the Theater of Marcellus.

facades consisting of four Corinthian columns topped by pediments, with an inscription on the architrave celebrating the Severian restoration. Two columns of the external facade are still standing, while the other two were replaced in the Middle Ages by an arch.

THEATER OF MARCELLUS

The project for the so-called Theater of Marcellus dates to Caesar's time, but the building was finished only in 13 BC by Augustus, who officially dedicated it in the name of his nephew Marcellus, his first designated heir who died prematurely in 23 BC. In the 13th century, the building was occupied by the noble Savelli family; in the 18th century it passed to the Orsinis. The refined Renaissance palace that occupies the third floor of the exterior facade of the cavea is the work of the architect Baldassarre Peruzzi. It has been calculated that the cavea (129.80 meters diameter) held between 15,000 and 20,000 spectators, making it the largest theater in Rome as far as audience capacity was concerned.

SYNAGOGUE

The Synagogue, or Israelite Temple, stands on Via del Portico di Ottavia, along the Tiber. Like other Italian synagogues, it is characterized by a style that can be best classified as "exotic revival," in this case Assyrian-Babylonian. The building terminates in a large aluminum **dome**, a clear indication of its belonging to the early twentieth century; in fact, the Synagogue was designed by the architects Armanni and Costa and built in 1904. As the presence of a Synagogue would indicate, the area in which it stands was once occupied by the Jewish ghetto.

Rome's synagogue.

In the Ghetto

A glimpse down a narrow street, the plaque recalling the rout of 16 October 1943, and the fountain by Landini, named the Fontana delle Tartarughe after Bernini's sculptures of tortoises were added in the 17th century.

A plaque in front of the church of Sant'Angelo in Pescheria, where in the 1500s Gregory VIII ordered compulsory sermons for the Jews, recalls the dramatic roundup by Nazi troops on 16 October 1943. Despite repeated demolition and reconstruction from the 1800s onward, these streets—once Rome's ghetto—still bear the signs of the persecution and restrictions that the Jewish community suffered here as elsewhere. But today, times have changed. The gates that at nightfall locked the Jewish families of the capital in the ghetto have been torn down, and the alleyways and streets bubble with life. Nor is there any lack of attractions for tourists. In the Sant'Angelo neighborhood—where Rome's ghetto was built in 1555 to separate the Jews from the gentiles, in the area today roughly delimited by Via del Portico d'Ottavia, Piazza delle Cinque Scole, and the Tiber river—the heart of Italy's oldest Jewish community, whose origins date back thousands of years, to the 2nd century BC, still beats strongly. And if, in Vicolo della Reginella, we can still imagine what the ancient ghetto, with its long-demolished tall homes, must have been like, the sense of hard-earned freedom that followed the temporary abolition of the ghetto in 1848 and its final demise when the Papal States were overthrown in 1870 is clearly expressed by the great synagogue on Lungotevere de' Cenci: Rome's premier synagogue, a majestic construction in an eclectic mix of Liberty and Middle Eastern styles, the well-loved "Tempio Maggiore" of the community. The monumental building, inaugurated in 1904, also houses the Rabbinical Office, the Spanish Temple, the Ritual Bath, the Historical Archive, and Rome's Jewish Museum.

Also of interest in the area is the small church of San Gregorio delle Divina Pietà, another sacred site where, over the centuries, the Jews were forced to listen to sermons targeting their conversion (in this regard, it is said that the most observant Jews came to church with their ears stopped with wax . . .). The facade still bears a bilingual inscription, in Hebrew and Latin, condemning the Jewish religion as perseverance in error.

The Sant'Angelo neighborhood is densely populated and oft visited by tourists, because the ancient traditions are still mirrored in the windows of the kosher shops, the typical trattorie that

propose well-known dishes of the Roman Jewish culinary heritage (for example, the exceptional fried foods: artichokes "alla Giudìa," squash flowers stuffed with mozzarella and anchovies, and salt cod), the pastry shops and bakeries—like the one near the Porticus of Octavia that has been open for 200 years!—where one can buy sweets recalling ancient flavors, braided risen loaves, honey biscuits, *torta di ricotta* cheesecake, and *visciole*, the special Jewish "pizza" filled with candied fruit and nuts—and of course, matzo bread.

On this page, the queue in front of an ancient bakery in Rome's Ghetto district and glimpses of a typical trattoria serving the incomparable artichokes of the *Agro romano*.

ISOLA TIBERINA

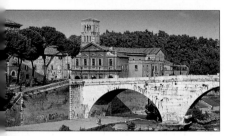

Ponte Rotto and a view of Ponte Cestio.

According to an old written tradition, the small island in the Tiber, now known as the Isola Tiberina, was formed when the grain that had been harvested in the Campus Martius was thrown into the river after the expulsion of the last Etruscan king of this line from Rome. The first important building erected on the island, the temple of Aesculapius, dates to 291 BC. Although nothing remains today of the original building, it is fairly certain that it stood on the same site as the 17th-century church of **San Bartolomeo**. The porticoes of the sanctuary of Aesculapius constituted a true hospital. Thanks to its being isolated from the inhabited areas, the medical tradition of the island continued through the Middle Ages and even in our times, with the Hospital of the Fatebenefratelli, adjacent to the small Church of San Giovanni Calibita. In antiquity, the island was joined to the city by two bridges. The bridge that still today connects the island to the left bank, near the Theater of Marcellus, is the ancient **Pons Fabricius**. The other bridge, by which the island communicates with Trastevere, is no longer the original one. The ancient **Pons Cestius** was torn down and partially rebuilt between 1888 and 1892. Downstream of the Isola Tiberina are the haunting ruins of the so-called **Ponte Rotto**, a bridge built on the remains of the ancient Roman Pons Aemilius of 179 BC. Some would date its origins to the 6th century BC, on the basis of its embankments. The span still standing in midstream dates to the late 16th century, although the pylons on which it rests are still those of the Roman bridge.

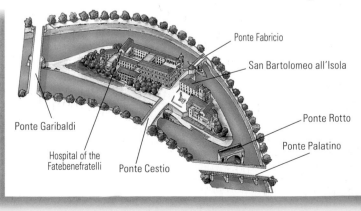

Ponte Fabricio

San Bartolomeo all'Isola

Ponte Rotto

Ponte Palatino

Ponte Garibaldi

Hospital of the Fatebenefratelli

Ponte Cestio

CHURCH OF SANTA CECILIA IN TRASTEVERE

The origins of this church, which stands at the back of a spacious courtyard, date back to the 5th century, when it was built on the remains of a Roman house said by some to be that of Saint Valerian, a martyred Roman patrician. The 18th-century **interior**, conserves at the center of the presbytery a marble *ciborium*, a 13th-century masterpiece by Arnolfo di Cambio and the marble statue of Saint Cecilia by Maderno (under the altar in the presbytery), and the mosaic of Paschal I in the semi-dome of the apse.

Santa Cecilia in Trastevere: detail of Pietro Cavallini's fresco of the *Last Judgement* (13th cent.).

Santa Maria in Trastevere: detail of the apse's mosaic, the *Presentation in the Temple* (13th cent.) by Cavallini.

SANTA MARIA IN TRASTEVERE

Possibly founded around 221 AD by Saint Calixtus (or so at least legend would have it), the church was completely rebuilt at the dawn of the second millennium and again restructured in the 18th century by Pope Clement XI. The simple 12th-century facade is splendid, with its three arched windows and fine mosaics from the same period. In the apse, at the height of the windows, are various outstanding mosaics by Cavallini narrating *Scenes from the Life of the Virgin*.

From top to bottom:
Aldo Fabrizi, a well-known
Roman actor
and gastronomist,
was a habitué
of Trastevere's
most picturesque
trattorie, two of
which are shown
below. Bottom,
the tiny Piazza
Trilussa.

Trastevere

*Trastevere has always been
considered a working-class
district. From the time of the
Republic it was inhabited by
Jewish and Syrian immigrants
and artisans, small traders,
sailors, and fishermen attracted
by the proximity of the Tiber
river port. In the Middle Ages,
Trastevere acquired new
streets and lanes that remain
the characteristic cornice for
churches of great artistic value.
Today, enlivened by trattorie,
pubs, charming small shops,
and markets, the district has
made a name for itself as one
of the capital's liveliest, day
and night.*

For many people, a Sunday visit
to the largest of
the Roman
markets is a
ritual, a leap
into the spar-
kling world of bargains, dis-
coveries, and even counterfeit goods.
Between Viale Trastevere and Porta
Portuense, in an area with a vocation
for trade, just a few steps from the
Tiber and in ancient times served by
intense river traffic, there's something
for everyone. New and used clothing,
of course, but also household articles,
plants and flowers, sandwiches with
the typical Roman *porchetta* roast
pork, second-hand bicycles and used
books, bags and purses, furniture, old
LPs and new CDs, old laces, umbrel-
las, toys, cosmetics, knick-knacks, and
antiques. Italy's oldest and most popular flea market is open every Sunday
from dawn to two in the afternoon.

piazza
di Porta Portese

CASTEL SANT'ANGELO

Castel Sant'Angelo was originally the *mausoleum of the emperor Hadrian*, designed and ordered built by Hadrian himself in 130 AD as his final resting place and that of all the members of the Antonine dynasty. The overall aspect of the construction was that of an immense tumulus grave, of Etruscan derivation and built on the model of the Mausoleum of Augustus. The sepulchral chamber at the center of the mausoleum, which housed the cinerary urns of the emperor and his family members and later those of all his successors up to Caracalla, was reached through a helicoidal gallery. Even

The bronze statue of the Archangel Michael atop the fortress.

Castel Sant'Angelo from the bridge of the same name, to which G. Bernini added statues of angels.

under Aurelian, in fact, the Hadrian's Mausoleum, while still preserving its role as a place of burial, had become part of the defensive system created to defend Ponte Helios, today's **Ponte Sant'Angelo**, which performed the function of access ramp to the mausoleum. In about 520, Theodoric transformed the building into a state prison, a role it was destined to play until 1901 (among others, Cellini and Cagliostro were held prisoners here). He also made it a fortress, to which use it was consecrated at the time of the Gothic War that bloodied Rome for a lengthy period. Some decades after the end of the conflict, in 590, the plague descended to afflict the city. Saint Gregory the Great was pope at the time; one day, as he crossed the bridge in front of

Castel Sant'Angelo: an aerial view of the fortress and the bridge.

the mausoleum, he saw at the summit of the conical roof an angel sheathing a flaming sword, which he took as a sign that the epidemic would soon cease. From that moment on the mausoleum/ fortress took the name of Castel Sant'Angelo, but only later, in 1544, was the episode commemorated with the installation of a marble statue of the *Archangel Michael* by Raffaello da Montelupo in the place the apparition had been seen. The original angel was replaced in 1752 by the bronze copy by Verschaffelt. During the Middle Ages, the fortress became especially important for defense of the Vatican, above all from the ninth century, when Pope Leo IV made it an integral part of that system of walls that delimited the area known as the "Leonine City" and that connected it to many other buildings, including the nearby Vatican Palace. In the 13th century, under Pope Nicholas III, an overhead corridor was added along this stretch of the

Castel Sant'Angelo from the Tiber.

walls. Known as the *"Passetto"* or the *Borgo Corridor*, it was restructured and perfected in the following centuries to permit the popes to reach Castel Sant'Angelo quickly in case of danger; the corridor was also used for secretly conducting prelates or nobles suspected of crimes into the prisons in the fortress. As part of the actions targeting improvement of the defenses of the Leonine City carried out in the late 15th century, the first pope of the modern age, Alexander VI, had Giuliano da Sangallo reinforce the castle with construction of *a four-sided surrounding with four octagonal corner towers* named for the four evangelists, a series of new bastions, and a wide moat. A few years later, under Julius II, the marble loggia overlooking the Tiber was added; Paul III, fearing a Turkish invasion of the coasts of Latium, commissioned Antonio Sangallo the Younger to completely restore the defensive

installations and to enlarge *the papal apartments* in the castle. The rooms were decorated by Perin del Vaga and his studio in the mid-sixteenth century with cycles of frescoes inspired by the history of the Church, as in the *Sala Paolina* (or Sala del Consiglio), and by figures from classical mythology, as in the rooms known as the *Camera del Perseo* and the *Camera di Amore* and *Psyche*. But for the most part, Castel Sant'Angelo still conserves the character of a fortress built for defense, with its armed bastions complete with batteries of cannon, the Armory of Clement X built by Bernini and later transformed into the Chapel of the Condannati the so-called "Oliare," large rooms and silos used to store foodstuffs for use in case of siege, and the parapet walk, which still today offers the visitor a full view of the Vatican and indeed a goodly portion of the city of Rome.

The straight-line thoroughfare of Via della Conciliazione leading to Saint Peter's Basilica.

Via della Conciliazione

This broad prospective thoroughfare leading to the majestic Saint Peter's Basilica was created in 1937; its construction forced demolition of a great part of the old and characteristic group of buildings known as the Spina dei Borghi. A number of very interesting buildings face onto this great thoroughfare, the name of which celebrates the reconciliation between the Italian State and the Church. The 15th-century **Palazzo dei Penitenzieri**, **Palazzo Torlonia**, the **Church of Santa Maria in Traspontina**.

VATICAN CITY

Vatican City lies between Monte Mario to the north and the Janiculum to the south. In Roman times, the area now covered by the small Vatican State was called the Ager Vaticanus and was occupied by a circus and by Nero's gardens. Since 1929, the year in which the Lateran Treaty was stipulated between the Holy See and the Italian State, Vatican City has been an independent sovereign state. In addition to being the head of the Apostolic Roman Catholic Church, the pope has full legislative, executive and judiciary powers. Vatican City is completely independent of the Italian state, even though the two maintain extremely friendly relations. The Vatican prints its own stamps and has its own railroad station and a well-known Italian-language newspaper, the *Osservatore Romano*, which is distributed throughout Italy. The city also has its own security service (once called the "pontifical carabinieri") and a real police force: the famous "Swiss Guards" who since the early 16th century have protected the person of the pope.

VATICAN GARDENS - An almost perfectly preserved, 16th-century style Italian formal garden.

FONTANA DELL'AQUILONE - Built by Giovanni Vasanzio, the fountain takes its name from the enormous tufa stone eagle atop the rock.

RADIO VATICANA - The first station was set up by Guglielmo Marconi in 1931, not far from today's studios, located in a bastion of the ancient Leonine Walls, once home to the astronomical observatory.

PALAZZO DEL GOVERNATORATO

SANTO STEFANO DEGLI ABISSINI - Founded by Leo II, the church was granted to the Coptic friars in 1479 by Pope Sixtus IV.

SACRISTY - Designed in the latter half of the 1700s by Marchionni for Pius VI as a freestanding building, it is joined to the basilica by two passageways. The rooms alongside contain the **Treasury of Saint Peter's**, a collection of the most precious ornaments and relics of the Vatican treasure (right: the Crux Vaticana, a 6th-century reliquary encrusted with gemstones) that survived the Saracen raids in 846, the Sack of Rome in 1527, and the Napoleonic confiscations. The Treasury also houses the Holy Column, a relic said to be a fragment of the Temple of Solomon in Jerusalem against which Jesus rested, a marvelous **ciborium by Donatello**, the **monument to Sixtus IV** by Pollaiolo, the sarcophagus of Giunio Basso (prefect of Rome converted to Christianity in 359), and the dalmatic said to have belonged to Charlemagne.

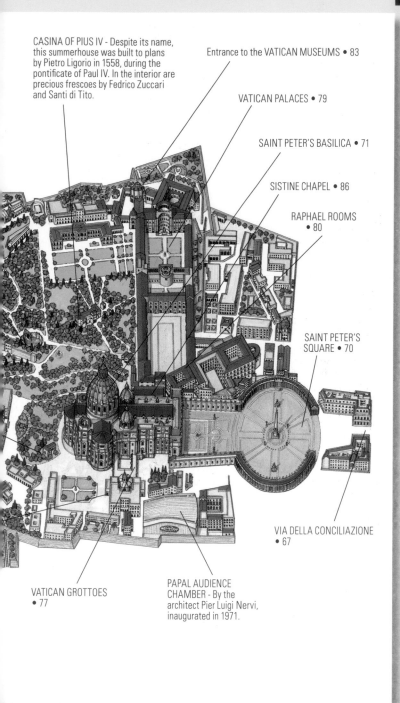

CASINA OF PIUS IV - Despite its name, this summerhouse was built to plans by Pietro Ligorio in 1558, during the pontificate of Paul IV. In the interior are precious frescoes by Fedrico Zuccari and Santi di Tito.

Entrance to the VATICAN MUSEUMS • 83

VATICAN PALACES • 79

SAINT PETER'S BASILICA • 71

SISTINE CHAPEL • 86

RAPHAEL ROOMS • 80

SAINT PETER'S SQUARE • 70

VIA DELLA CONCILIAZIONE • 67

VATICAN GROTTOES • 77

PAPAL AUDIENCE CHAMBER - By the architect Pier Luigi Nervi, inaugurated in 1971.

An view of Saint Peter's Square and Via della Conciliazione from the roof of the basilica.

PIAZZA SAN PIETRO
(SAINT PETER'S SQUARE)

The square was built over a part of the ancient Vatican Circus (or Nero's Circus, though actually built by Caligula), of which there remains the so-called **Vatican Obelisk**, transported here in 37 AD from Alexandria, where it decorated Caesar's Forum. Called in medieval times the *aguglia*, it stood at length beside the basilica, until 1596, when Sixtus V ordered Carlo Maderno to move it to its present site. In 1613, Paul V bid the same Maderno build a fountain to its right; half a century later, a "twin" fountain by Carlo Fontana, placed symmetrically with respect to the first, was added. Again under Sixtus V, the origi-nal bronze globe that topped the obelisk (today in the Capitoline Museums) and that was believed to contain the ashes of Caesar was replaced with that pope's family emblem, the mountains and the star, topped by a crucifix containing a fragment of the Holy Cross of Christ's Crucifixion. In the mid-17th century, when the monumental work of rebuilding Saint Peter's Basilica was well-delineated, attention naturally shifted to the square before it. The fervent activity then being concluded provided the impetus for the sumptuous design of the square, which was built by Gian Lorenzo Bernini between 1656 and 1667.

BASILICA DI SAN PIETRO
(SAINT PETER'S BASILICA)

In the classical period, Nero's Circus stood on what is now the site of Saint Peter's, between the Tiber, the Janiculum, and the Vatican hill. Saint Peter, the Prince of the Apostles, was martyred and then buried here in 64 AD. Pope Anacletus had a small ad corpus basilica, or a simple shrine, built here. In 324, the emperor Constantine replaced the presumably modest shrine with a true basilica. The original Saint Peter's was completed in 349 by Constantius, son of Constantine, and over the centuries was embellished and renovated by donations and the restoration work carried out by the popes and munificent princes. It was in Constantine's basilica that Charlemagne received the crown from the hands of Leo III in 800; Lothair, Louis II, and Frederick III were also crowned emperors after him. Even so, a thousand years after its foundation, Saint Peter's was falling into ruin. In 1452, Pope Nicholas V, on the advice of Leon Battista Alberti, appointed Bernardo Rossellino to renovate and enlarge the Basilica to the latter's plan. Work was not resumed until 1506, under Pope Julius II della Rovere, and this time the planned intervention was radical. Most of the original church was dismantled by Bramante (who earned himself the title of maestro ruinante), who intended building a "modern" building in the Classical style, from the ground up, on a Greek-cross plan inspired by the Pantheon. Various architects and works supervisors - Fra' Giocondo, Raphael, Giuliano da Sangallo, Baldassarre Peruz-

Aerial view of Saint Peter's Square and Bernini's colonnade.

zi, and Antonio da Sangallo the Younger - succeeded each other until about the middle of the century until finally, in 1547, Michelangelo was appointed by Paul III. Needless to say, Michelangelo followed his own interpretation of Bramante's plan: he modified and simplified it in part, and designed a soaring **dome** (originally hemispherical) to crown the renovated basilica. Michelangelo was succeeded by Vignola, Pirro Ligorio, Giacomo Della Porta, and Domenico Fontana, all of whom interpreted Michelangelo's ideas quite faithfully. Then, under Paul V, it was decided to expand the basilica and return to the Latin cruciform plan. With this in mind, the architect Carlo Maderno added three chapels to each side of the building and brought the nave as far as the present **facade**, the building of which was entrusted to him when he won an important competition.

A spectacular view of Saint Peter's Square from the top of the dome of the basilica.

The facade of Saint Peter's Basilica and Michelangelo's soaring dome.

Work on the facade was begun in November of 1607 and terminated in 1614, after having absorbed mountains of "travertine from Tivoli." After the death of Carlo Maderno in 1629, the next director of works was Gian Lorenzo Bernini, who left his unmistakable mark on the building: the prevalently Baroque character it now displays was his doing. It is sufficient to mention the erection of the justly-famous bronze **Baldacchino** (begun in 1624 and inaugurated on Saint Peter's Day in 1633) over the Papal Altar, the decoration of the piers of the dome with four large statues, and, of course, the placing of the *Throne of Saint Peter* at the back of the apse. This is one of Bernini's most sumptuous inventions, a truly marvel-

ous machine built around the old wooden chair which a pious tradition says was used by the apostle Peter. The layout of Saint Peter's Square, once more by Bernini, also dates to the papacy of Alexander VII (who financed the works for the throne). It was instead under Clement X that the architect designed and built the small round temple which is the tabernacle of the Chapel of the Sacrament. Any number of chapels, all splendid in one way or the other, line the perimeter of Saint Peter's Basilica: to begin with, the **Chapel of the Pietà**, named after Michelangelo's famous marble sculpture of the *Pietà* made between 1499 and 1500, when the artist was still a young man, for Cardinal Jean de Bilhères. After the **Chapel of**

Saint Peter's Basilica, Bernini's "Gloria" with the *Cathedra Petri* or Throne of Saint Peter at its center.

Saint Sebastian (which contains Francesco Messina's *Monument to Pope Pius XII*) comes the better-known **Chapel of the Holy Sacrament**, with the tabernacle by Bernini and the elaborate bronze railings designed by Borromini; next is the **Gregorian Chapel**, a late 16th-century work completed by Giacomo della Porta and heavily decorated with mosaics and precious marbles, the **Colonna Chapel**, the sumptuous **Chapel of the Choir**, the **Chapel of the Presentation**, with the recent *Monument to Pope John XXIII* by Emilio Greco. Saint Peter's Basilica infact contains a whole collection of famous monuments, from Michelangelo's *Pietà* to the venerated 13th-*century effigy of Saint Peter*

The Swiss Guard

When the Pontifical Swiss Guard was instituted, in 1506, the Swiss Confederation had already been loaning its troops, who were widely known as excellent mercenary soldiers, to European courts in exchange for foodstuffs and trade privileges. The Vatican guard unit was created to counter the threat of aggression against the Papal State from outside forces. Contrary to all expectations, during an extremely violent engagement at the time of the Sack of Rome (1527) the Swiss Guard was routed and massacred by the united Spanish and Lansquenet (German mercenary) forces, who had penetrated into the Vatican to the Raphael Rooms, which they sacked. New guards are sworn in every year on May 6, the anniversary of this battle. Today, the duties of the Guard are to stand guard in certain areas of the Vatican palaces and to defend the pope during liturgical ceremonies and as he moves within the Vatican and travels outside its walls. Candidates applying to serve in the Guard must be single male Swiss citizens of the Roman Catholic faith, between 19 and 30 years of age, and must meet the height requirement of 1.74 meters. The minimum term of service is two years. It is commonly accepted that the sumptuous, Renaissance-looking dress uniform of the Guard, with its ample pleats, was designed by Michelangelo.

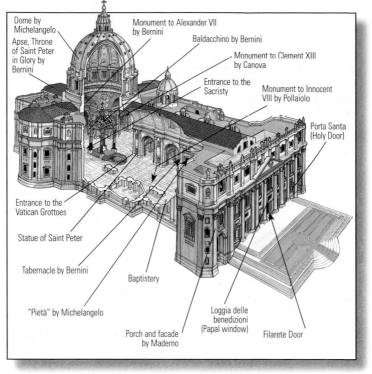

Dome by Michelangelo

Monument to Alexander VII by Bernini

Baldacchino by Bernini

Apse, Throne of Saint Peter in Glory by Bernini

Monument to Clement XIII by Canova

Entrance to the Sacristy

Monument to Innocent VIII by Pollaiolo

Porta Santa (Holy Door)

Entrance to the Vatican Grottoes

Statue of Saint Peter

Tabernacle by Bernini

Baptistery

"Pietà" by Michelangelo

Loggia delle benedizioni (Papal window)

Filarete Door

Porch and facade by Maderno

shown in the act of blessing, to Bernini's funeral *monument to Pope Urban VIII*, the analogous funeral *monument to Pope Paul III*, by Guglielmo Della Porta, the *bronze tomb* created by Antonio Pollaiolo *for Pope Innocent VIII*, and the Neoclassical *Stuart*

A view of the monumental interior of Saint Peter's Basilica.

Monument by Canova. The great sacristy rises before the left transept. As large as a church, and in fact originally conceived as an independent building, the sacristy consists of the **Sagrestia Comune** on an octagonal central plan, the so-called **Sacristy of the Canons**, and the **Chapter Hall**. It was all designed by the Roman architect Carlo Marchionni at the behest of Pius VI, who laid the first stone in 1776. Annexed to the basilica is the **Museo della Fabbrica di San Pietro**, or Historical Artistic Museum, which includes the *Treasury of Saint Peter's*. It was designed by Giovan Battista Giovenale and contains what remains of the enormous artistic patrimony of the church which was repeatedly broken up and carried off during the Saracen raids, the Sack of Rome in 1527, and the Napoleonic confiscations.

Bernini's celebrated "Baldacchino" over the papal altar.

VATICAN GROTTOES

The grottoes, situated under the nave of Saint Peter's Basilica, contain the tombs of many popes, as well as early Christian sarcophagi, architectural fragments and various monuments from the Basilica. The area embraces two sections, known as the "New Grottoes" and the "Old Grottoes."

The tomb of Saint Peter.

Michelangelo in Rome

Michelangelo's work in Rome is an essential aspect of the land-scape of the papal capital, which the artist interpreted in all its grandeur as no other before or since. From the plans for **Piazza del Campidoglio** and **Porta Pia**, and the final plan for **Saint Peter's Basilica**—from Michelangelo architect—to the important sculptural group of the *Pietà* (1499-1500), a fixture and attraction of the basilica, to the **Sistine Chapel** frescoes, everything he did in Rome speaks of an artist capable of conceiving and carrying out large-scale projects in harmony with the wishes of his patron—in this case the papacy—who saw him as the true heir of classical art: "Gloria del secolo nostro" as he was defined by Pope Paul III. Michelangelo (Caprese M. 1475 - Rome 1564) was invited to Rome in 1508 by Pope Julius II della Rovere to fresco the **vault** of the Sistine Chapel, which until his time had been decorated with gold stars on a blue field. Creation of what is considered Michelangelo's greatest masterpiece and the city's best-known work of art cost the artist years of backbreaking work alone on special scaffolding, and conflicts with the papal court as he attempted to wrest maximum freedom of artistic expression from his patrons. 1515 is the date of the gigantic statue of **Moses** in the basilica of San Pietro in Vincoli, a complement to the **Mausoleum of Julius II** della Rovere commissioned by the pope before his death. Michelangelo returned to Rome in 1534, during the pontificate of Clement VI de' Medici, to fresco the end wall of the Sistine Chapel with the famous *Last Judgment*. The artist lived in the Eternal City until his death, supported by a life stipend granted by Pope Paul III Farnese.

Saint Peter's Basilica, the *Pietà* by Michelangelo.

VATICAN PALACES

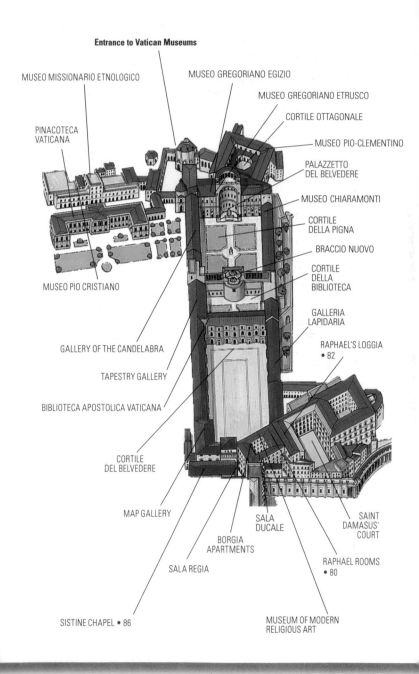

Entrance to Vatican Museums

MUSEO MISSIONARIO ETNOLOGICO

MUSEO GREGORIANO EGIZIO

MUSEO GREGORIANO ETRUSCO

CORTILE OTTAGONALE

MUSEO PIO-CLEMENTINO

PINACOTECA
VATICANA

PALAZZETTO
DEL BELVEDERE

MUSEO CHIARAMONTI

CORTILE
DELLA PIGNA

BRACCIO NUOVO

CORTILE
DELLA
BIBLIOTECA

MUSEO PIO CRISTIANO

GALLERIA
LAPIDARIA

RAPHAEL'S LOGGIA
• 82

GALLERY OF THE CANDELABRA

TAPESTRY GALLERY

BIBLIOTECA APOSTOLICA VATICANA

CORTILE
DEL BELVEDERE

MAP GALLERY

SALA
DUCALE

SAINT
DAMASUS'
COURT

BORGIA
APARTMENTS

RAPHAEL ROOMS
• 80

SALA REGIA

SISTINE CHAPEL • 86

MUSEUM OF MODERN
RELIGIOUS ART

Stanza della Segnatura (Signature Room), *The School of Athens* and, bottom, *The Dispute of the Blessed Sacraments.*

RAPHAEL ROOMS

The master began frescoing what are now known as the Stanze di Raffaello (Raphael Rooms) in 1509. The work, which continued into the following years under Leo X, revolves around themes that celebrate the power of Faith and the Church. The first room to be frescoed was the **Stanza della Segnatura**, or Signature Room, called thus because it was here that the pope signed official documents; Raphael's sure touch

Details of the decoration on the walls of the Raphael Rooms.

gleams from all the frescoes in this magnificent room, from *the Dispute of the Blessed Sacraments*, depicting the glorification of the Eucharist, to the *School of Athens*, where within a grandiose architectural frame the wise men and the philosophers of ancient times are set side by side with the seigneurs and the artists of the Renaissance cultural scene, all gathered around the figures of Plato and Aristotle, and to the Parnassus, an allegorical celebration of the arts impersonated by the mythological figures of the Muses and the pagan gods. In the alternating medallions and panels of the ceiling, almost as though to offer a symbolic compendium of the frescoes on the walls below, Raphael painted a number of allegorical representations of the *Sciences and the Arts* (*Theology, Justice, Philosophy, Poetry, Astronomy*) together with emblematic episodes referred to them (*Adam and Eve*, the *Judgement of Solomon, Apollo and Marsyas*). Between 1512 and 1514, Raphael worked on the decoration of the **Room of Heliodorus**, where he frescoed historical episodes in accordance with an iconographic program dictated by Julius II: Leo I Halting Attila, alluding to the Battle of Ravenna in 1512 at which the future Leo X defeated the French; the *Miracle at Bolsena*, illustrating the institution of the *Corpus Domini* by Urban IV and also calling to mind the vow made by Julius II before the siege of Bologna; the biblical episode of the *Expulsion of Heliodorus from the Temple*, which refers to the pope's struggle against the enemies of the Church; and finally the *Liberation of Saint Peter*, alluding to the liberation of Leo X, who was imprisoned following the Battle of Ravenna. The next two years were dedicated to the **Room of the Fire** in the Borgo, which takes its name from the principal fresco, The Borgo Fire of 847 AD, inspired by the figure of Leo IV who quenched the fire by making the sign of the Cross. This fresco and the -other three in the room (the *Battle of Ostia*, the *Oath of Leo III*, the *Coronation of Charlemagne*), executed almost entirely by Raphael's pupils under the strict guidance of the master, make specific reference

to the illustrious predecessors of Leo X, during whose pontificate the room was decorated, who bore his same name.

The **Sala dei Palafrenieri** also contained wall paintings by Raphael, which were destroyed and later replaced by other frescoes ordered by Gregory XIII in the late 1500s. The decoration of the **Hall of Constantine**, instead, is certainly the work of one of Raphael's most important followers, Giulio Romano. Following the death of the master he led a team of artists who illustrated in fresco episodes from the life of Constantine: the *Baptism of Constantine*, the *Battle of the Milvian Bridge*, the *Apparition of the Cross*, and *Constantine's Donation*.

RAPHAEL'S LOGGIA

One of the most significant corners in the entire Vatican palace complex, the lovely, airy loggia was begun by Bramante but terminated by Raphael in about 1518. Twelve of the 13 bays with pavilion vaults (an inspired architectural solution) are frescoed with scenes from the Old Testament, while the last is decorated with stories of the New Testament.

The frescoes, all exhibiting an extreme freshness and an imaginative use of perspective, are the work of some of Raphael's most illustrious pupils, such as Giulio Romano, Polidoro da Caravaggio, Giovanni da Udine, Perin del Vaga, Pellegrino Aretusi da Modena, and Vincenzo da San Gimignano.

A detail of *The School of Athens.*

Stanza di Eliodoro (Heliodorus Room), *The Expulsion of Heliodorus from the Temple* and a detail of the episode.

VATICAN MUSEUMS

The new architecture of the entrance to the Vatican Museums and a detail of the portal by Cecco Bonanotte.

From the very first, the complex that is today called the Palazzi Vaticani and that is the result of a long process of construction and transformation has hosted splendid collections of art assembled by the various popes, including the celebrated **Pinacoteca Vaticana**. The buildings gradually became museums to all effects; the first step in this direction was taken in the latter half of the eighteenth century by Clement XIV, who transformed the Palazzetto del Belvedere into the museum that following the reorganization ordered by Clement's successor Pius VI took the name of **Museo Pio-Clementino**. In the first half of the following century, that passion for archaeology and antiquity that was a hallmark of Neoclassical taste induced two popes, Pius VII and Gregory XVI, to create one of the cardinal institutions of the Vatican museum complex: the former was responsible for the foundation of the **Museo Chiaramonti**, to the decoration of which even Canova contributed and for which the so-called Braccio Nuovo was expressly built in 1816; the latter, instead, organized the **Museo Gregoriano Etrusco** and the **Museo Gregoriano Egizio** in seventeen rooms. Later on in the nineteenth century, Pope Leo XIII, to whom we owe restoration of numerous of the myriad parts making up the Vatican complex, opened to the public many rooms which theretofore

New Entrance to the Vatican Museums

The new entrance to the Vatican Museums, that was opened in 2000 has provided a rational solution for coping with the ever-increasing number of people who visit the museum complex.

The construction work involved the creation of a new, four-storey building between the 18th century Museo Pio-Clementino and the old 16th century walls. A broad, **helicoidal ramp** that is 165 meters long leads visitors to the exhibition rooms via the Cortile delle Corazze that was covered by a glass and metal roof.

Two images of the gracious spiral ramp leading to the exhibition rooms of the Vatican Museums.

had been reserved for the pope and the highest members of the ecclesiastical hierarchy. The first such revelation was the Borgia Apartments, the rooms of which later became the seat of the **Collection of Modern Religious Art** inaugurated by Pope Paul VI in 1973. The creation of new museums went on all through the twentieth century: John XXIII had both the **Museo Missionario-Etnologico**, instituted in 1926 to house the material exhibited at the Missionary Exhibit of the 1925 Jubilee, and the **Museo Pio Cristiano,** founded in 1854 by Pius IX to organize the paintings, inscriptions, reliefs and sculptures from the catacombs and the ancient Roman basilicas.

MICHELANGELO IN THE SISTINE CHAPEL

Michelangelo, the famed master of the Sistine Chapel, completed his frescoes in two phases: the period between 1508 and 1512 was employed in painting the **vaults** under commission by Pope Clement VII, whereas his other masterpiece, the ***Last Judgement***, was commissioned by Pope Paul III (Alessandro Farnese) for the back wall of the chapel nearly a quarter of a century later. These two frescoes, which together cover a surface of approximately 800 square meters, represent perhaps the greatest artistic achievement of all time.

General view and two details of Michelangelo's ceiling frescoes in the Sistine Chapel.

SISTINE CHAPEL

Between 1475 and 1481, under Pope Sixtus IV Della Rovere, Giovannino de' Dolci built what may be called the "Chapel of Chapels" to plans by Baccio Pontelli. Architecturally, the Sistine Chapel is a spacious rectangular hall with a barrel vault, divided into two unequal parts by a splendid marble *transenna* or screen by Mino da Fiesole, Giovanni Dalmata and Andrea Bregno. The same artists also made the Cantoria.

But the chief attractions of the Sistine Chapel are of course its frescoes, particularly those by Michelangelo

on the walls and vault. Michelangelo's marvelous paintings postdate those covering the wall facing the altar and the two side walls, painted during the pontificate of Sixtus IV (between 1481 and 1483) by Perugino, Pinturicchio, Luca Signorelli, Cosimo Rosselli, Domenico Ghirlandaio, and Botticelli.

At that time the vault was blue and strewn with stars, and so it remained until Julius II commissioned Michelangelo to redecorate the vast surface.

*B*eginning from the rear left, The twelve frescoes around the vault are of **Sibyls** and **Prophets**. Above these figures, softly rendered **nudes** support festoons and medallions. In the center, nine pictures depict the **Stories of the Genesis**. Beginning from the one above the altar, they are: *God dividing the light from the darkness, God creating the sun, the moon, and plant life, God dividing the waters and the land and creating the fishes and the birds,* the incredibly famous *Creation of Adam,* the *Creation of Eve from Adam's rib,* the *Temptation* and the *Expulsion of Adam and Eve from the Garden of Eden,* the *Flood,* and the *Drunkenness of Noah.*

*T*wenty-five years later, between 1536 and 1541, Michelangelo returned to the Sistine Chapel, this time under the papacy of Paul III Farnese. His great new fresco of the **Last Judgement** covers the whole back wall of the Sistine Chapel; it is so large that two of Perugino's earlier frescoes had to be destroyed and two large arched windows walled up.

Michelangelo, ceiling of the Sistine Chapel: *Original Sin and the Expulsion of Adam and Eve from Paradise* (top), and the *Creation of Adam* (bottom).

Details of the side-wall frescoes: in the lunettes, Michelangelo's "Ancestors of Christ" and, beneath, four figures from the "Popes" cycle.
In the lower register, two 15th-century frescoes, *Christ Giving the Keys to Saint Peter by Perugino* and Cosimo Rosselli's *Last Supper.*

Left, Michelangelo's *Last Judgement.*

Below, *Scenes from the Life of Moses* by Sandro Botticelli and *Moses' Journey into Egypt* by Perugino.

The main facade of the basilica of San Giovanni in Laterano.

BASILICA OF SAN GIOVANNI IN LATERANO

Originally built by Constantine, plundered by the Genseric's Vandals, frequently sacked, damaged by the earthquake of 896 and various fires - for most of its existence, the Basilica of San Giovanni in Laterano has been the object of reconstruction and restoration. The balustrade above the attic supports the colossal statues of *Christ, Saints John the Baptist and John the Evangelist*, and the *Doctors of the Church*. There are five entrances (the last to the right is known as the *"Porta Santa"* and is opened only in Jubilee years), each surmounted by a loggia. The *statue of Emperor Constantine* was brought here from the Baths of Diocletian. The majestic **interior** is a Latin cross with a nave and two aisles on either side. The great conch of the apse at the back of the Basilica is covered with mosaics dating to the 4th, 6th, and 13th centuries (note, in particular, the figures of the *Apostles* signed by Jacopo Torriti). Above the organ, a large 19th-century fresco by Francesco Grandi depicts episodes concerning the *Founding and Construction of the Basilica*. The decoration of the transept also deals with analogous subjects (including the Conversion of Constantine); it was completely restored during the pontificate of Clement VIII by the architect Giovanni della Porta and the painter known as the Cavalier d'Arpino. Under the Cavalier d'Arpino's fresco of the *Ascension of Christ* is the gilded bronze pediment, supported by antique bronze columns, that protects the *altar of the Chapel of the Holy Sacrament* designed for Clement VIII by Pietro Paolo Olivieri and supporting a precious ciborium.

Among the many other chapels built in various periods as further decoration for the basilica are the **Colonna Chapel**, also know as the Choir Chapel, by Girolamo Rainaldi (1570-1655); the **Chapel of the Crucifixion**, which preserves a fragment of the presumed *Funeral Monument of Nicholas IV* attributed to Adeodato di Cosma (13th century); the **Chapel of Massimo**, by Giacomo della Porta; the **Torlonia Chapel**, quite different from that preceding it and splendidly decorated in neo-Renaissance style by the architect Raimondi (1850); and the architecturally-complete and self-sufficient **Corsini Chapel**, built on the Greek-cross plan by Alessandro Galilei for Clement XII. A corridor leads to the **Old Sacristy**, with the *Annunciation* by Venusti and a *Saint John the Evangelist* by the Cavalier d'Arpino, and to the **New Sacristy**, with a 15th-century *Annunciation* of the Tuscan school. In the nearby Cosmatesque **Cloister**, a 13th-century work by Vassalletto, are visible remains of the most ancient portion of the Basilica.

Opposite page, one of the twelve statues of Apostles that line the nave.

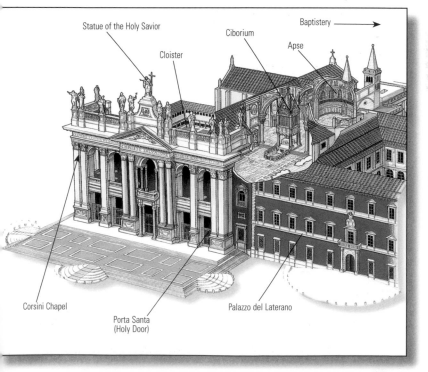

Statue of the Holy Savior

Cloister

Ciborium

Baptistery →

Apse

Corsini Chapel

Porta Santa (Holy Door)

Palazzo del Laterano

Palazzo del Laterano. In the foreground, the tallest (31 m) and oldest Egyptian obelisk in Rome, moved here from the Circus Maximus. In the background, the side entrance to the basilica.

PALAZZO DEL LATERANO

Built for Sixtus V by the architect Domenico Fontana on the site of the ancient Patriarchio, the residence of the Popes from Constantine until the papacy was transferred to Avignon (1305). The magnificent palace, on which work began in 1586, was conceived as a summer residence for the papal court, which was then moved to the Quirinal.

Baptistery of Saint John - Originally raised by Constantine, the baptistery was completely reconstructed a number of times; the building we see today dates to the 17th century. It is also known as San Giovanni in Fonte or in Laterano. The structure is that of the prototype Christian baptistery.

SCALA SANTA

The Palazzo del *Sancta Sanctorum* owes its name to the fact that was originally designed to contain, or incorporate, the Popes' Chapel (or Sancta Sanctorum). Pope Sixtus V commissioned the palace from the architect Domenico Fontana, who built it in 1585-1590. The Chapel was originally part of a building known as the "Patriarchio" (7th - 8th centuries) that at the time housed the papal court. The name of "Scala Santa" derives from the erroneous identification of one of the staircases of the Patriarchio as the flight of stairs in Pilate's *Praetorium* ascended by Christ when he was judged by Pilate. Nowadays, the term Sancta Sanctorum is used to indicate the **Chapel of Saint Laurence**, overflowing with relics and at the same time a true jewel of Cosmatesque art with its tabernacles along the walls and its mosaic ceiling.

Top right, the Scala Santa.

SAN PIETRO IN VINCOLI

This is without doubt one of the most venerated minor basilicas in Rome, rich as it is in the memory of the first Pope of the Church, from whom it received its name. It is also called the Basilica Eudoxiana, after the wife of Emperor Valentinian III. Eudoxiana, upon receiving from her mother the chains that had bound St. Peter during his imprisonment in Jerusalem, donated them to Pope St. Leo I. When the pope set these chains with the ones that had bound the wrists and ankles of St. Peter in the Mamertine Prison, he saw the two **chains** unite to form a single piece. This relic is still kept here and the old Latin name of church, '*in vinculis*', has remained.

In the right transept is the major attraction of the church, the unfinished **Mausoleum of Julius II** by Michelangelo with the imposing figure of Michelangelo's *Moses* in the center.

Basilica of San Pietro in Vincoli, Michelangelo's tomb of Julius II with the statue of *Moses* at the center. At the sides, left, the statue of *Rachel* (personifying the "contemplative life"); right, *Leah* ("active life").

Moses, prophet and leader of the Jews during the exodus from ancient Egypt to the promised land, is portrayed by Michelangelo as he severely regards the idolatrous Jews while holding in his right hand the Tables of the Law received on Mount Sinai.

The two small horns over his head allude to the light which, according to the Bible story, shone from his forehead after the divine revelation.

"And it came to pass, when Moses came down from Mount Sinai . . . Moses wist not that the skin of his face shone while he talked with Him."
(Exodus 34:29)

Domus Aurea

The imperial villa, the magnificent residence that Nero built after the great fire that destroyed Rome in 64 A.D. extended over an area of 80 hectares, that is, nearly the entire center of Rome. All that remains today of the lavish palace is 150 rooms of the portion on **Colle Oppio** centered on the fulcrum of the entire complex, that is the octagonal room. The most important and striking rooms include the **nymphaeum** with the mosaic of *Ulysses Offering a Cup of Wine to Polyphemus*, the **room with the golden ceiling**, the **room of Hector and Andromache**, the **room of Achilles at Skyros**, and, of course the **Octagonal Room**. The accidental finding of the Domus Aurea at the end of the 15th century led to the discovery of ancient Roman paintings by Fabullo, an artist known for his austere style, distinguished by his use of colors azure, cinnabar, dark red, indigo and green. Renais-

sance artists such as Raphael, Pinturicchio and Ghirlandaio visited what was then visible of the Domus Aurea and from it drew inspiration for their masterpieces.

Nero's Domus Aurea in a fanciful 17th-century reconstruction.

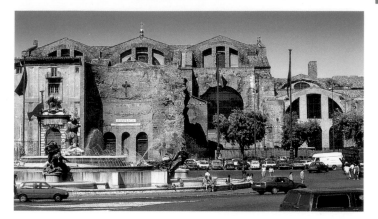

The remains of the Baths of Diocletian seen from Piazza Esedra.

BATHS OF DIOCLETIAN

The Baths of Diocletian were in all probability the largest *thermae* ever built in Rome. They went up in a relatively brief period of time, between 298 and 306 AD, under the two Augustan tetrarchs Diocletian and Maximinian, as the dedicatory inscription reminds us. A special branch of the old **Aqua Marcia** aqueduct supplied water for the enormous cistern (91 meters in length), which was demolished once and for all in 1876. Reference to these baths is still to be found in the name "Termini" by which the nearby railroad station is now known. The structures of the original complex of buildings were greatly modified , but the original layout is in part still legible. The main bath building was at the center of a rectangular enclosure with a large semicircular exedra on one of the long sides (corresponding to what is now Piazza della Repubblica), two rotundas at the corners and numerous hemicycles along the perimeter. The plan of the main building is along the lines of the great imperial baths: a large central basilica, the *calidarium-tepidarium-frigidarium* complex on the median axis of the short side, and *palaestrae* and accessory services balancing each other on either side. The Baths of Diocletian are home to a section of the **Museo Nazionale Romano**.

Baths of Diocletian, Museo Nazionale Romano: the Octagonal Hall.

The basilica of Santa Maria Maggiore seen from above.

BASILICA
OF SANTA MARIA MAGGIORE

In August of 352 AD, snow miraculously fell on the Esquiline hill, and in it Pope Liberius traced the perimeter of the first church on the site, popularly called Santa Maria della Neve (Our Lady of the Snow). The present Church of Santa Maria Maggiore was completely rebuilt by Sixtus III (432-440). The basilica was neither restored nor rebuilt until the 12th century, when Eugene III had a portico built for the facade, much like those still standing in San Lorenzo fuori le Mura or in San Giorgio al Velabro. At the end of the 13th century, Nicholas IV promoted the

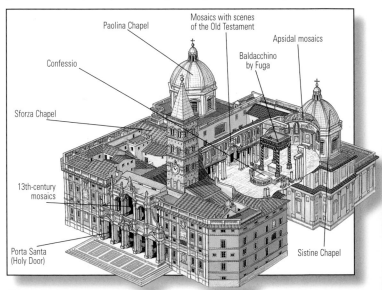

Paolina Chapel

Mosaics with scenes of the Old Testament

Apsidal mosaics

Confessio

Baldacchino by Fuga

Sforza Chapel

13th-century mosaics

Porta Santa (Holy Door)

Sistine Chapel

Santa Maria Maggiore, the cupola of the Sistine Chapel and the mosaic of the *Coronation of the Virgin* (13th cent.) in the apse.

Below, the interior of the Pauline Chapel.

renovation of the apse. Only in the 18th century did Clement XII, after having demolished the old portico, entrust the creation of a new facade to Ferdinando Fuga. Now giving the impression of being squeezed between the two tall flanking buildings (dating to the 17th and 18th centuries), the **facade** is preceded by a vast flight of steps and features a portico with an architrave on the ground floor and a loggia with arches above; the whole is crowned by a balustrade which curiously extends on either side of the facade to define the twin palaces at the sides. Rich sculptural decoration runs along the front and under the portico, while the loggia of the upper floor, (13th century), still preserves the mosaic decoration of the older facade. The **interior** is on a tripartite basilica plan with forty Ionic columns supporting an entablature with a mosaic frieze. The coffered *ceiling* is commonly attributed to Giuliano da Sangallo, while, the pavement is in Cosmatesque marblework, although much of it was restored under Benedict XIV.

Palazzo del Quirinale preceded by the obelisk flanked by two massive Dioscuri from the Roman era.

PIAZZA DEL QUIRINALE

This large square, which in a sense represents the "noble" center of Rome, is overlooked by some of the most interesting buildings of Renaissance, Baroque and rococo Rome (such as the Palazzo del Quirinale, the Palazzo della Consulta, the Church of Sant' Andrea al Quirinale); the fourth, open side is delimited by a theatrical balustrade graced by Roman statues.

PALAZZO DEL QUIRINALE

Among the architects who worked on the Palazzo del Quirinale were Martino Longhi, Domenico Fontana, Carlo Maderno, Gian Lorenzo Bernini, and Ferdinando Fuga, who was also the architect for the Palazzo della Consulta between 1732 and 1734. The Quirinale was the seat of the papacy from Clement XII to 1870, the year in which the complex was chosen as the palace of the kings of united Italy; since 1947 it has been the official residence of the president of the Italian republic.

CHURCH OF SAN CARLO ALLE QUATTRO FONTANE

Purely Baroque in its layout, this stunning work by Borromini dates to the middle of the 17th century. The almost "undulating"

facade, extremely innovative for the period, catches the light in an inspired play of *chiaroscuro*.

FONTANA DEL TRITONE

The curve facade of San Carlo alle Quattro Fontane by Borromini.

Still another fascinating fountain by Gian Lorenzo Bernini is that which has stood at the center of Piazza Barberini since 1643, famous for the apparent lack of any kind of architectural support for the statue of the *Triton* from which it takes its name. He is in fact supported by a scallop shell that in turn rests on the arched tails of four dolphins; the spray of water that animates the whole ensemble is naturalistically blown upwards by the Triton through a conch.

The Fontana del Tritone at the center of Piazza Barberini.

The facade of Palazzo Barberini.

PALAZZO BARBERINI AND THE
GALLERIA NAZIONALE D'ARTE ANTICA

The rooms of the palace are the showcase for the Roman statues and antiquities amassed by the Barberini family over the years and to a fine picture collection that is today the nucleus of the **Galleria Nazionale d'Arte Antica** founded in 1895. The absolute masterpiece of this collection, which includes, among many others, works by Filippo

Festival in Honor of Queen Christina of Sweden at the Palazzo Barberini by Filippo Lauri (1656).

Lippi, Perugino, Bronzino, Tintoretto, Guido Reni, Guercino and many foreign masters, is Raphael's *La Fornarina*, in which criticism traditionally sees the portrait of the woman the artist "loved until his death." Particular interest also invests the *Judith and Holophernes* by Caravaggio and the *Narcissus* for many years attributed to the Baroque painter but now believed by criticism to have been painted by one of his pupils.

Besides the picture gallery, the palace also sported a library and, above all, many architectural features conceived to support its role as a reception facility. Among these were the famous theater designed by Pietro da Cortona, a spheristerion (no longer existing), and the immense space in front of the building in which fêtes and carrousels were held.

Via Veneto

Galleria Nazionale d'Arte Antica:
the *Annunciation* by Filippo Lippi
and, below, the *Heitz Madonna*
by Giulio Romano.

When people reach Via Veneto they barely glance at the beautiful **Fountain of the Bees** by Bernini, the seventeenth century churches of **Santa Maria della Concezione** and **Sant'Isidoro**, the nineteenth century **Boncompagni Ludovisi** palazzo or the twentieth century buildings of the **Ministero dell'Industria e del Commercio** and the **Banca Nazionale del Lavoro** that recall the transformations Marcello Piacentini brought about in the Rome of the Fascist era. In the world's imagination Via Veneto is quite something else, and the credit goes to Fellini, and his famous film, *La Dolce Vita*. In the 1960s, with a meticulous reconstruction In Cinecittà he brought this elegant, sophisticated street into the limelight and launched it as the meeting place for the world of film, VIPs In general and also as a potential launching pad for aspiring actors and movie stars.

Even today Via Veneto is an open air salon as well as the living monument to a glorious period in the history of Italian filmmaking. Tourists never miss a chance to walk down the street, especially towards evening, at cocktail time. They admire the elegant shops and the new, trendy places such as the *Hard Rock Café*, but, inevitably, their eyes seek out the *Hotel Excelsior* where Hollywood's most important producers have stayed, and then they sit down in the most famous cafés, recalling when a seductive, and perhaps barefooted, Anita Ekberg walked by. It is still possible to see celebrities on the Via Veneto because the myth lives on.

The bee, symbol of the Barberini family,
in a detail of Bernini's Fontana delle Api
at the start of Via Veneto.

PIAZZALE DON MINZONI

VIA G. DE NOTARIS

ALE DELLE BELLE ARTI

VIALE BRUNO BUOZZI

B PIAZZALE DI VILLA GIULIA

VIA GRAMSCI

B

VIA DI VILLA GIULIA

19

18

VIA G. MANGILI

VIA OMERO

VIA ALDOVRANDI

VIALE DELLE BELLE ARTI

B

PIAZZALE CERVANTES

VIALE DEL GIARDINO ZOOLOGICO

16

1

VIA DI VILLA GIULIA

VIALE MADAMA

VIA MADAM LETIZIA

21

20

17 **15**

VIA DI CAV

14

VIA DEGLI ORTI GIUSTINIANI

VIA DI VILLA RUFFO

VIA A. FERRERO

PIAZZA FIOCCO

VIALE CANONICA

PIAZZA DI SIE

VIA FLAMINIA

VIA WASHINGTON

VIA FIORELLO LA GUARDIA

VIALE DEL LAGO

VIALE DEL MURO TORTO

VIA CASINO DI RAFFAELLO

13

B M Flaminia **1**

VIALE VALADIER

VIALE DELLE MAGNOLIE

VIA GOETHE

Porta del Popolo

PINCIO

PIAZZA NAPOLEONE I

PIAZZALE DEI MARTIRI

GALOPPATOIO

VIALE SAN PAOLO DEL BRASILE

PIAZZA DEL POPOLO

VIA G. D'ANNUNZIO

PIAZZA BUCAREST

VIALE MEDICI

22

VIA DEL CORSO

VIA MARGUTTA

VIALE TRINITÀ DEI MONTI

VIALE DEL MURO TORTO

P

VIA DEL BABUINO

VIA DI PORTA PINCIANA

B

VIA MARIO DE FIORI

B M Spagna

PIAZZA DI SPAGNA

TRINITÀ DEI MONTI

VIA LOMBARDIA

VIA LUDOVISI

VIA CONDOTTI

VIA SISTINA

VIA CRISPI

VIA DEGLI ARTISTI

VIA BORGOGNONA

PIAZZA MIGNANELLI

VIA FRATTINA

1 Greek Gateway
2 Borghese Gallery
3 Garden of Venus
4 Aviary (Uccelliera)
5 Sun dial house
6 Water tower
7 The Sarcophagi Avenue
8 Theatre Prospect
9 Secret Gardens
10 Biopark
11 Civic Museum of Zoology
12 Marine Horses Fountain
13 Temple of Diana
14 The Clock House
15 Temple of Antonino and Faustina
16 Graziano's House

17 Canonica Museum
18 National Museum of Modern Art
19 Etruscan Museum, Villa Giulia
20 Temple of Aesculapius
21 Arch of Septimus Severius
22 Valadier House

VILLA BORGHESE

*The villa and its park were designed for Cardinal Scipione Caffarelli Borghese in the early 1600s; although the villa was completely remodeled at the end of the following century. The **park** is the largest in the city, all of six kilometers around its perimeter, and it is also the loveliest and the most fascinating. In the midst of luxuriant plant life and a wealth of decorative elements lies a small artificial lake surrounded by an elegant garden known as the **Giardino del Lago.** An Ionic **temple** dedicated to Aesculapius, built in the late 18th century, rises on the island at the center. A little further on are evocative avenues leading to **Piazza di Siena,** designed as an amphitheater. Every year horse-lovers gather here to watch one the most famous equestrian events in the world.*

Villa Borghese: the Casino Borghese, residence of Cardinal Scipione. Below, the "Garden of Venus" at the rear of the villa.

→ ENTRANCE
B BUSES
M UNDERGROUND
P CAR PARK

MUSEUM AND GALLERY

The green slope of the Pincio overlooking Via Flaminia, delimited on the side toward the city center by the Aurelian Walls, was chosen in 1608 by Cardinal Scipione Borghese-as the site for a suburban villa immersed in an enormous park.

The recently-restored *palazzina*, also called the **Casino Borghese**, hosts the **Museo** and the **Galleria Borghese**, two of the most celebrated art collections in the world. Both got their start with Cardinal Scipione, who brought together not only many paintings but also antiquities of different origin and entrusted their restoration to the greatest artists of the time.

Bust of *Scipione Borghese* by Gian Lorenzo Bernini.

First and foremost among these masters was Gian Lorenzo Bernini (1598-1680), who also created for his rich benefactor certain among the absolute masterpieces of Baroque statuary: the *David*, sculpted in 1623-1624, whose countenance is the self-portrait of the artist, and *Apollo and Daphne*, a marble group sculpted during the same period but of mythological inspiration, as was the *Rape of Proserpine*, an early but brilliant work. In 1807, Prince Camillo Borghese sold the collection to his cousin, Napoleon Bonaparte, who carried off many pieces to the Louvre where they still form the main nucleus of the classical antiquities section. Two years earlier, Camillo's wife Pauline had been portrayed by Canova in the pose of *Venus*, a work that still today is one of the major attractions of the museum.

The *Rape of Proserpine* by Gian Lorenzo Bernini.

Other works by Bernini
at the gallery: *David*,
with details of the head,
and *Apollo and Daphne*.

*Paolina Borghese Bonaparte as Venus
Victrix* by Antonio Canova.

Lorenzo Lotto,
Holy Conversation.

RENAISSANCE PAINTING

Like the collection of statues and antiquities, the collection of paint-ings Like the collection of statues and antiquities, the collection of paintings that today graces the **Galleria Borghese** was also begun by Cardinal Scipione, who assembled a great number of masterpieces by the most illustrious exponents of 16th- and 17th-century painting. Caravaggio is represented here with some of his most interesting and most evocative works: the *Boy with a Fruit Basket*, one of the master's first Roman works, the *Little Bacchus*, the *Madonna dei Palafrenieri*, *Saint Jerome*, and the *David with the head of Goliath*, one of his last works, in which the slain giant wears his countenance. Alongside the works by the great Baroque artist from Lombardy, Cardinal Scipione collected paintings of enormous value by Raphael (the *Entombment*

Titian (Tiziano Vecellio), *Sacred and Profane Love* (left);
Giorgione, (attrib.), *Singer with Flute.*

of Christ, perhaps better known as the *Borghese Deposition*), Titian (*Sacred and Profane Love*), and painters of the Ferrarese school (*Apollo* by Dosso Dossi). Later acquisitions (including the addition of the collection of Olimpia Aldobrandini, wife of Paolo Borghese) brought to the gallery such masterpieces as the *Virgin and Child with Young Saint John and Angels* by Botticelli, Correggio's *Danaë*, the *Portrait of a Man* by Antonello da Messina and works by many other Italian and foreign masters (Domenichino, Lorenzo Lotto, Parmigianino, Veronese, Rubens, and Cranach).

Three works by Caravaggio, from top to bottom: *Saint Jerome, Sick Little Bacchus, Boy with a Fruit Basket.*

Villa Borghese: the Giardino del Lago with the Temple of Aesculapius.

VILLA GIULIA AND THE ETRUSCAN MUSEUM

One of the most fanciful realizations of architectural Mannerism is Villa Giulia, built for Pope Julius III in the area called the Vigna Vecchia against the walls of the city. Villa Giulia was chosen in 1889 to house the rich collection of **Etruscan antiquities** and relics of the Italic civilizations that flourished between the Iron Age and the beginning of Roman hegemony in the territory between the lower Tiber valley and Tuscany.

Museo Etrusco di Villa Giulia: an Attic amphora depicting Achilles and Ajax throwing dice.

Right and bottom, the head of Leucothea, "white goddess" of the sea (terracotta, 4th cent. BC) and the *Husband and Wife Sarcophagus* (6th cent. BC), both from Pyrgi near Cerveteri.

Museo Etrusco di Villa Giulia: head of Silenus, fictile antefix from Pyrgi.

Aranciera di Villa Borghese, Museo Carlo Bilotti: Giacomo Manzù, *Cardinal* (bronze, h. 300 cm) and, bottom, Giorgio De Chirico, *Hector and Andromache* (bronze, h. 230 cm).

ARANCIERA DI VILLA BORGHESE

The Aranciera di Villa Borghese (Orangery), which predates Cardinal Scipione Borghese's villa, has been modified and enlarged many times over the course of its centuries of history. Today, its first floor hosts the **Museo Carlo Bilotti**, named for the donor of the collection displayed here, while the ground floor is a splendid venue for temporary exhibits.

The Aranciera.

The facade and the quadriporticus.

BASILICA OF SAN PAOLO FUORI LE MURA

Built by Constantine over the tomb of the apostle Paul, the church remained standing until 15 July 1823, when it was gutted by fire. It was not reconsecrated until 1854. The **facade** rising above the quadriporticus is rich-ly decorated with mosaics both in the gable (the *Blessing Christ with Saints Peter and Paul*) and in the frieze (an *Agnus Dei* on a hill that rises up symbolically between the two holy cities of Jerusalem and Bethlehem), and with the four large *Symbols of the Prophets* alternating with the three windows.

In the **interior** two stately stat-ues of Saint Peter and Saint Paul overlook the raised transept with the sumptuous triumphal arch dating to the time of Leo the Great, called the Arch of Galla Placidia, which frames the apse and which was already decorated with mosaics in the 5th century. In the 13th cen-tury the mosaics were replaced by Honorius III, who employed Venetian craftsmen sent for the purpose to the pope by the doge of Venice. Objects housed in the basilica include the Gothic *Ciborium* made by Arnolfo di Cambio in 1285 in collabo-ration with a certain "Petro" who some believe to have been Pietro Cavallini, the equally pre-sumed author of the *mosaics* (of which only fragments remain) now decorating the reverse side of the arch of triumph and once part of the decoration of the exterior of the Basilica. Under the exquisite canopy of Arnolfo's tabernacle is the altar over the *tomb of Saint Paul* with the inevitable *fenestrella con-fessionis* (confessional window) through which can be seen the fourth-century epigraph reading "Paulo Apostolo Mart."

Top, an aerial view of Porta San Paolo and the Pyramid of Caius Cestius enclosed in the Aurelian Walls. Bottom, the Baths of Caracalla.

PORTA SAN PAOLO AND THE PYRAMID OF CAIUS CESTIUS

What is now known as Porta San Paolo is one of the best preserved of Rome's city gates (the other is Porta San Sebastiano) in the formidable circuit of the **Aurelian Walls**. The rooms inside the building now house the **Museo della Via Ostiense**.

A curious funeral monument of the early Imperial period, the **Pyramid of Caius Cestius**, was raised next to *Porta Ostiensis* during the construction of the Aurelian walls. The building was obviously inspired by Egyptian models, of the Ptolemaic period rather than that of the pharaohs, as was fashionable in Rome after the conquest of Egypt in 30 BC.

BATHS OF CARACALLA

The Baths of Caracalla are a magnificent, and excellently-preserved, example of thermae from the Imperial period. Construction was begun by the emperor Caracalla in 212 AD. The baths continued to function until 537 when, during the siege of Rome by Vitiges and his Goths, the aqueducts of the city were cut off. In the 16th century, excavations carried out in the enormous building brought to light various works of art including the *Farnese Bull* and the *Hercules*, now in the National Museum of Naples. The *mosaics of athletes* that decorated the hemicycles of the large side courtyards of the thermae were discovered in 1824 (now in the Vatican Museums).

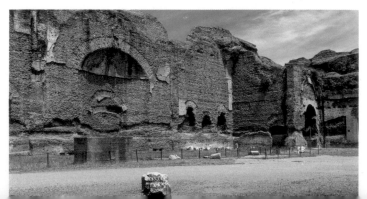

VIA APPIA ANTICA

The most important of the Roman consular roads, known as the Regina Viarum (the queen of roads), begins at Porta San Sebastiano and winds towards the interior bordered with ancient and not-so-ancient monuments. Miraculous events such as the famous episode of "Domine quo vadis?" are thought to have taken place along this thoroughfare.

SAN GIOVANNI A PORTA LATINA
PORTA LATINA
CHURCH OF "DOMINE QUO VADIS?"
BASILICA DI SAN SEBASTIANO
Jewish Catacombs
TOMB OF CECILIA METELLA
CIRCUS OF MAXENTIUS
Catacombs of Domitilla
Catacombs of St. Calixtus
Catacombs of St. Sebastian

CHURCH OF "DOMINE QUO VADIS?"

The church known by this famous phrase actually seems to have been dedicated to *Santa Maria in Palmis*. But the world-wide fame of the building rests less on its artistic merits than on Christian tradition, which relates that the site on which the church stands was the spot where Jesus appeared to Peter as he was fleeing Rome for fear of being crucified. The apostle, taken aback, uttered the famous phrase *"Domine quo vadis?"* (Lord, where are you going?); Jesus is said to have answered *"Venio iterum crucifigi"* (I am returning to be crucified). Peter grasped the implicit invitation in Christ's words and returned to Rome and martyrdom.

Catacombs of San Callisto - These catacombs are among Rome's best known, having been developed by Pope Calixtus III and become the official burial ground for the bishops of Rome. The catacombs extend for about 20 kilometers on four different levels and have been only partly explored. The part open to the public includes the *Crypt of the Popes*, where several of the early popes were buried.

Catacombs of Domitilla - Also known as the Catacombs of Santi Nereo e Achilleo, this network of tunnels is the largest in Rome and traditionally developed from a simple family burial ground that belonged to Domitilla, the wife or niece of the consul Flavius Clemens put to death by Domitian.

Tomb of Cecilia Metella - This sumptuous and typically Roman mausoleum was originally built in the late republican period for Cecilia, the wife of Crassus and daughter of Quintus Metellus, the conqueror of Crete. It was modified in 1302 by the Caetani family, who adapted it to perform defensive functions for their neighboring castle. Even so, the *cella* of the ancient tomb, with its conical covering, can still identified.

Catacombs

These deep galleries were once quarries for travertine and *pozzolana* stone. Situated on the outskirts of Rome, they became meeting places for the early Christians and shortly thereafter were also used as cemeteries (1st - 4th centuries). Following many centuries of abandon, the catacombs were rediscovered and reappraised in the 16th century. The most suggestive portions of the vast maze of tunnels that spreads out to the sides of the Via Appia go by the names of **Domitilla**, **San Callisto**, **San Sebastiano**, **Sant'Agnese** and **Santa Priscilla**.

Catacombs of San Callisto, the painting of the Good Shepherd in the Crypt of Lucina and a view of the Crypt of Santa Cecilia.

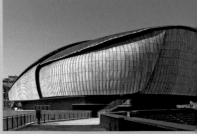

THE AUDITORIUM - PARCO DELLA MUSICA BY RENZO PIANO

Since 2002, music can be enjoyed in the new auditorium, the music park designed by Renzo Piano where architectural and sound quality are permanently bonded and that has been defined as "architecture that plays music." The new complex extends over an area of 55,000 square meters and comprises three main buildings of different sizes. The three concert halls, "sound boxes" as they have been called, radiate around the outdoor theater set in a huge, tree-shaded park. The first is a concert hall named for **Saint Cecilia**, patron saint of musicians; it has a seating capacity of 2800 and is designed for big symphony concerts. The **Sala Sinopoli**, for an audience of 1200 hosts all types of events, from contemporary music to ballet. The **Sala Petrassi**, with 700 seats, is perfect for opera, chamber music, Baroque music, plays and films. The foyer can also host concerts. However it is the outdoor **amphitheater**, named for Luciano Berio, with seats for up to 3000 spectators that is the heart of the auditorium.

The Parco della Musica Auditorium between the bank of the Tiber and the Parioli hill: a view of the open-air hemicycle theater and the elegant profile of one of the three concert halls.

Three suggestive views of the 20th-century Palazzo della Civiltà del Lavoro.

EUR

This famous district, at one and the same time among the most recent and the most historical, was originally conceived as the site of the Esposizione Universale di Roma that was scheduled to have been held in 1942. Designed by a group of famous architects (Pagano, Piccinato, Vietti and Rossi) coordinated and directed by Marcello Piacentini, it covers an area of 420 hectares in the shape of a pentagon. The formative concept was that of monumentality, and the district was developed with a view to the future expansion of Rome toward the Tyrrhenian Sea. Among the significant paradigms of Italian architecture of the first half of the 20th century are the **Palazzo della Civiltà del Lavoro** and the buildings housing the **Museo Preistorico-Etnografico Pigorini**, the **Museo dell'Alto Medioevo**, the **Museo delle Arti e Tradizioni Popolari**, and the **Museo della Civiltà Romana**. Opening soon in this historic district, the new **Centro Congressi Italia convention center** on an area of 27,000 square meters.

The plans, by architect Massimiliano Fuksas, call for innovative logistics solutions for the complex and use of high-tech construction materials.

Cinecittà

Cinecittà is an Italian myth from the nineteen sixties and even today it is a significant player on the economic scene. It was established during the fascist era, in the Thirties that was both a period of crisis for Italian cinema and the time when intellectuals supported movies as an important propaganda tool. After a fire destroyed the Cines studios in 1935, the government decided to build a real cinema city, designed by the architect Peressuti, on a Roman countryside estate along the Via Tuscolana.

Cinecittà was inaugurated in 1937. Work was lively until the 'forties, then came the collapse, the layoffs and the Nazi occupation that transformed the studios into holding pens for civilian prisoners; then after the Liberation it was used to shelter refugees. "Cuore" directed by Duilio Coletti (1947) was the first film produced to launch the recovery and a new round of successes: it was with "Quo vadis" by Mervyn LeRoy (1951) and William Wyler's "Ben Hur" (1959) that Cinecittà became **"Hollywood on the Tiber"** and its highly competitive studios brought wealth to post-war Rome. The myth developed when, thanks to the successes of mainly American movies, Rome became the prime a destination for the world's show business celebrities. The paparazzi followed famous movie stars and directors through the city's hotels and cafés, society events of all types filled gossip columns and beautiful girls flocked there from all over Italy pursuing the dream of a contract. And the wealth flowed through the economy, because the city of movies needed walk-ons, bit players, craftsmen, costume designers and seamstresses, and technicians of all types to meet the needs of continuous growth.

Federico Fellini's film "La dolce vita" was the symbol of this renewal, and this new way of life in Rome: it was the beginning of a long series of successes. More than one thousand movies were made at

Cinecittà from 1937 on, and it became part of cinematic history thanks to Federico Fellini, Luchino Visconti, Roberto Rossellini and then the most famous American filmmakers, who even today admire and use the new technological facilities in Rome, including Mel Gibson who shot "The Passion of Christ" here. Cinecittà has adapted to changing times, it now works with the latest generation digital systems, but even today creativity is its trump card.

Images that have become symbols of Italian moviemaking: the Lancia Aurelia B24 convertible, the third star of Il Sorpasso (The Easy Life, 1962, directed by Dino Risi) and Anita Ekberg in an immortal pose in the waters of the Trevi fountain in Federico Fellini's La Dolce Vita (1960).

The Castelli Romani in a Bottle

Of volcanic origin, the area of the Castelli Romani boasts well-drained soils rich in potassium that are ideal for fructification of renowned wine-grapes and achieving high sugar content. Vine-growing is an ancient tradition in these hills: it began in ancient times, in the feudal period, and was perpetuated when the papacy assigned land as a bonus to the most valorous returning soldiers. The stars in the vineyards are white grape varieties, from **Bellone** *to* **Bonvino**, *from* **Malvasia** *Bianca di Candia to local Malvasia ("del Lazio" or "Puntinato"), from the yellow* **Trebbiano** *to the green: all grapes eminently suitable for producing high-quality table wines. Among the most widely cultivated red wine-grapes are* **Cesanese, Merlot, Montepulciano, Sangiovese**, *and the so-called* **Nero Buono** *or Nero di Cori. The wines that have always been—and still are—made from these grapes, most of which straw-colored with a delicate taste, have always been the protagonists of outings to the Castelli featuring stops at the traditional "fraschette," the typical country inns at which, in the past, a "frasca" or leafy bough on the facade indicated that the wine produced by the farms was sold by the glass to the public.*

The DOC area.

ROMA

GALLICANO
COLONNA
ZAGAROLO
GENAZZANO
FRASCATI
MONTE PORZIO CATONE
CIAMPINO
MONTECOMPATRI
GROTTAFERRATA
ROCCA PRIORA
MARINO
ROCCA DI PAPA
CASTEL GANDOLFO
ALBANO LAZIALE
ARICCIA
LARIANO
GENZANO
POMEZIA
LANUVIO
VELLETRI
CORI
ARDEA
APRILIA
CISTERNA DI LATINA

The Wines of the Castelli Romani

The DOC Wines

The area boasts a great number of DOC (Denominazione di Origine Controllata: "Controlled Denomination of Origin") wines. The earliest to earn this appellation (all now renowned and briefly described below) have been joined more recently by wines of the generic "Castelli Romani" DOC class and several excellent IGP (Indicazione Geografia Protetta: "Protected Geographic Indication") table wines. This system supports the producers who make single-grape wines or who produce red and rosé wines in areas where traditional regulations cover only whites.

Frascati - This wine, which is exclusively white, is produced in the towns of Frascati, Monte Porzio Catone, Grottaferrata, and Montecompatri, and in several other areas around Rome. Wine types are Frascati Normale Secco DOC (dry), Frascati Amabile DOC (medium sweet), and Cannellino and Frascati Superiore, Spumante (sparkling), and Novello (new, or last vintage). The alcohol content must be at least 11%; the color, intense straw yellow; the aroma, vinous with a delicate scent.

Montecompatri-Colonna - Produced in the towns of Montecompatri and Colonna, and in areas of the territories of Rocca Priora and Zagarolo, the Montecompatri-Colonna Bianco DOC is a pleasingly dry, straw yellow wine with never less than 11% alcohol content.

Velletri - The Velletri wine production area covers the towns of Velletri and Lariano and parts of Cisterna di Latina (LT). Velletri Bianco DOC may be Secco, Amabile, Superiore, Dolce (sweet), or Spumante, and the alcohol content of all versions is in excess of 11.5%. Velletri Rosso DOC is instead a fine red wine available in the Amabile and Riserva versions.

Colli Lanuvini - Produced in the territories of Genzano di Roma and Lanuvio in Secco, Amabile, and Dolce versions, this wine is straw yellow in color with golden highlights, a sapid taste, and a minimum alcohol content of 11%. Area wines with alcohol content in excess of 11.5% are classified as Colli Lanuvini Superiore DOC.

Colli Albani - This wine is produced in the territory embracing Albano, Ariccia, Castel Gandolfo, and Pomezia, in the Secco, Amabile, Superiore, Spumante, and Novello versions. Straw yellow in color, dry, medium-sweet, or sweet in flavor, the Colli Albani wines have a minimum alcohol content of 11%; wines with alcohol content exceeding 11.5% are denominated Colli Albani Superiore DOC.

Marino - The Marino wine production area extends through the territories of Marino, Castel Gandolfo, and Rome. The wine is available in the Secco, Amabile, Superiore, and Spumante versions. Delicate and straw-colored, Marino wines must have at least an 11.5% alcohol content; wines exceeding this limit are denominated Marino Superiore DOC.

Zagarolo - This wine is produced in Zagarolo and Gallicano in the Amabile and Superiore versions. The alcohol content exceeds 11.5%, the color is straw yellow, and the taste is smooth.

Roma at the Table

Partly of popular inspiration, partly created for the boards of the aristocrats and the popes (as the proverb runs, "If you want to learn to eat, you have to go to the   priests . . ."), Roman cuisine has retained all its genuine excellence through the centuries and even today has not been contaminated by the winds of globalization. Tourists will delight in unadulterated, tasty dishes based on the products of the farms of the fertile Agro romano (Roman plain) and the region's sheep and cattle stock-farms. All in all, the recipes fit the mold of the "Mediterranean diet"; although perhaps fattier than most, using heavier condiments, Roman specialties are nevertheless characterized by absolutely typical flavors, like that of the aromatic mentuccia (basil thyme, known in other regions as nepitella) or the grated pecorino cheese that here tops pasta in place of the Parmesan more widely used in the north. People used to say, "You can eat well anywhere in Rome"—and it's still true!

Bucatini all'Amatriciana

For the purists, let us start out by saying that this "typical Roman" dish actually originates in Abruzzo (Amatrice, today in the province of Rieti, once owed its allegiance to L'Aquila) and that, originally, it was "poor man's" fare prepared by the shepherds and not numbering tomato among its ingredients. But by now it is considered a Roman specialty par excellence; tourists are generally indifferent to its history but not to the taste of the "red" version as prepared in the capital's trattorie. Bucatini (thick tubular spaghetti) are served with a special tomato sauce incorporating onions sautéed with minced guanciale (streaky bacon made from pig's cheek) and topped at the last second with a cascade of grated pecorino cheese over the steaming pasta. Unique aromas and flavors, plus the consistency of a just-as-special pasta, always religiously cooked al dente.

Gnocchi alla romana

These tiny dumplings are an internationally-known dish with a delicate flavor. The basic ingredient is semolina, cooked in milk and then mixed with egg yolks and cheese and spread on a board to cool. The slab is cut into disks that are placed in a baking pan, topped with curls of butter and grated Parmesan cheese, and heated in the oven until the top is browned and crusty.

Spaghetti alla carbonara

The origins of this famous, robust first course, while not extremely ancient, are hotly debated. Some say this nutritious dish was invented by charcoal burners and woodsmen to replenish their energies after a day of grueling work; others attribute it to a chef affiliated with the 19th-century Carbonari secret political society; some even cite a similar recipe published in 1837 in a Neapolitan cookbook by the Duke of Buonvicino, Ippolito Cavalcanti. Whatever its origins, the rich sauce is based on lightly-sautéed *guanciale*, egg yolks, and an abundant dose of grated pecorino cheese.

Rigatoni con la "pajata"

This is a rich and yet delicately-flavored, authentically Roman dish that like many others—notably Coda alla Vaccinara—is strictly linked to use in ancient popular cooking of the *quinto quarto* (literally, the "fifth quarter"); that is, the part of the animal sniffed at by well-to-do customers who were more interested in the "noble" cuts of meat (the *quattro quarti*). This recipe is based on the small intestine of suckling calf, still containing the very nutritious, creamy chyme (partially digested milk). Cleaning and preparing the *pajata* for cooking is a time-consuming, complex procedure. Suffice it to say that the small intestine is cleaned and washed, cut into pieces, and tied off in rounds to as to prevent the chyme from escaping; the pieces are then sautéed with vegetables and herbs and spices (onion, garlic, celery, carrots, cloves, hot pepper, oil, salt and pepper); white wine is added and when it has evaporated tomato purée is added and the whole is simmered for about one hour. The resulting, highly flavorful sauce is traditionally served over rigatoni pasta, and the dish is completed with a dusting of grated pecorino cheese.

IL CUOCO CONSIGLIA. RIGATONI CON PAJATA!!

Pasta and Legumes

Over the centuries, popular cuisine has turned the legume from a staple (rich in plant proteins, legumes have always been considered the "poor man's meat") to a treasure. Legumes were matched with pasta or added to pasta cooked in broth to create filling one-dish meals with all the needed nutrients. The ancient Romans were especially fond of different kinds of *farinata* (a sort of porridge) made with legumes, and of thick cereal-based soups—the same dishes that, with their unique flavors

and nutritional qualities, are making such a comeback today. The menus of Rome's trattorie abound in ancient and traditional dishes that pair pasta with chick peas, beans, potatoes, broccoli . . . and in the thinner soups, the addition of tasty tidbits of pork (ham, bacon) and lard often enriches these already nutritious first courses with fats and new flavors.

Abbacchio

The Roman *abbacchio* is suckling or baby lamb, under 10 kilos in weight, which in ancient times was slaughtered or "*abbacchiato*" during the Easter season by a stroke of the club or *baculum*. Other sources insist that the name derives from the Latin diminutive *abecula*, from *ovecula* and *ovis*, sheep. In ancient times, *abbacchio* was holiday fare. The lambs and kids supplied to the city markets by the shepherds of the *Agro* were prepared as they still are today: cut in pieces, braised or stewed at length with rosemary and sage and a dash of vinegar, terminating with an addition of filleted anchovies that melt into the pot liquor. A delicious dish, typical of the Roman spring season. The Romans also make use the organ meats of the lambs, the *coratella* (liver, lungs, and heart), cooked with artichokes, parsley, and lemon.

Coda alla Vaccinara

This is a very tasty, popular dish that originated in the Rome's Regola neighborhood, where the *vaccinari* (who slaughtered, butchered, and skinned oxen) were located. Housewives of the time were experts in the use of the *quinto quarto*: as explained above, the parts of the animal that remained after sale, to the well-to-do customers, of the more prized parts of the carcass (the *quattro quarti*). The *coda* or tail—together with the kidneys, tripe, feet, and other variety meats—was a "poor" cut ennobled by the imagination of the cooks, who with it invented a dish that is still a sought-after favorite. Cut into joints and parboiled, the tail pieces are then sautéed in lard with carrots, onions, celery, and garlic, and seasoned with a pinch of cinnamon and nutmeg; red wine is added and evaporated, and the meat is allowed to stew for hours with tomato purée, marjoram, and water as needed. When the meat is tender, sticks of celery (Rome's "*sellero*"), blanched and flavored with pine nuts, raisins, and a little of the pan liquor from the meat, are added to the pot (some trattorie propose an interesting version with a touch of bittersweet chocolate). A complex dish, and a long time in the cooking (about 4 hours), that is eminently worth tasting.

Saltimbocca alla Romana

Pellegrino Artusi, celebrated author of *Scienza in cucina e l'arte di mangiar bene (Science in the Kitchen and the Art of Eating Well)*, tells us that *saltimbocca* were a Roman specialty as early as the late 1800s. This dish is easy to prepare: all that's really needed is a little care with the cooking. A small slice of veal, topped with a slice of prosciutto ham and a leaf of sage, all held together with a toothpick, is sautéed with butter, first on one side for about two minutes and then on the other. The trick is not to overheat the side with the prosciutto, which otherwise would toughen. The *saltimbocca* are removed from the pan and kept warm while the pan drippings are deglazed with water and more butter, allowed to thicken, and then drizzled over the meat for serving.

Artichokes: Carciofi "alla Giudìa" and "alla Romana"

Artichokes are a favorite vegetable in local gastronomy. The tradition of the Roman Jewish community (Italy's most ancient) gives us the recipe for fried artichokes, called "carciofi alla Giudìa," a dish that was served in the Roman ghetto to break the fast of Yom Kippur, the Day of Atonement, a day of total fasting dedicated entirely to contemplation and prayer. Now as in ancient times, the artichoke of choice is the *mammola*, a large globe variety typical of the Lazio region. The artichoke is trimmed but left whole, with a stub of stem, and fried upside down in oil until crisp and opened like a flower. Just as tasty, but very different, are artichokes prepared "alla Romana": left whole as in the preceding recipe but without the stem, they are set upright and a filling of minced garlic, *mentuccia*, and parsley is forced down between the leaves before baking in a slow oven with oil, salt, pepper, and water.

Misticanza, pinzimonio, and puntarelle

Even before they came into vogue in the rest of Italy, bowls of *misticanze* (mixed salad) of baby lettuces, wild greens, and *rughetta* (rucola) graced tables in Rome and the Lazio region in the spring. Wild salad greens are found almost everywhere: remember that the Roman legionnaires ate mainly fava beans, pecorino cheese, and greens, and that still today the sites of their camps are marked by spontaneous growths from plants first seeded in ancient times. Another ancient Roman custom is the *pinzimonio*: the vegetables that abounded in the *Agro*, served raw for dipping in oil and salt. As for chicory (wild endive), it is traditionally consumed blanched, squeezed to remove excess moisture, and sautéed with hot pepper and garlic ("*cicoria pazza*") or used for preparing "*acqua cotta*" soup with herbs and vegetables like mentuccia, potatoes, leeks, and fava beans. *Cicoria catalogna* is the source of the famous *puntarelle*, hollow shoots cut lengthwise, curled in ice-water, and topped with a dressing made of crushed garlic, anchovies, vinegar, olive oil, and salt and pepper, just as in Roman times.

Tortino di indivia

This delicious *savory pie made with anchovies and endive* is a dish from the Roman Jewish tradition. The ingredients—anchovy filets and endive leaves—are placed in alternating layers in a baking pan and sprinkled with oil, salt, and pepper; slow cooking, first on the stovetop and then in the oven, results in formation of a sort of pie, crusty on the top and tender inside, with its own special flavor.

Castagnole, maritozzi, and beignets

Roman cuisine includes few traditional sweets, if we exclude the *crostata di ricotta* (ricotta tart), the Christmas *pan giallo*, and the renowned *maritozzi*, typical sweet rolls with raisins and candied fruit that can be found at any pastry shop as a breakfast specialty. The latter, with their allusive name—which would seem to be a pejorative of *marito*, husband—are traditionally given as a joke to young women about to be married.

Castagnole, a specialty in Rome during the Carnival period, are chestnut-sized balls of dough made with flour, eggs, sugar, butter, leavening, and flavorings (lemon or wine or rum), fried and dusted with sugar. The *bigné di San Giuseppe* are flavored with lemon and filled with crème patissière: they were once sold on the streets on 19 March, the feast of Saint Joseph but also the pagan feast marking the end of the long winter season.

Ricotta and pecorino

In a region like Lazio, where sheep-raising has always been an important activity, ricotta and pecorino cheese are quality products, suitable for eating as is as a perfect cap to a meal or for use as an ingredient in a thousand recipes. We have already mentioned the *crostata di ricotta*, a typical dessert with a short pastry crust and a rich, aromatic filling of ricotta cheese whipped with egg yolks, sugar, grated citrus rind, raisins, pine nuts, candied fruit, and cinnamon. A variant of this recipe is *bocconotti*, in which ricotta blended with eggs, cinnamon, and candied fruit is spread between two layers of short pastry to form little tarts or a single larger dessert.

Pecorino Romano has boasted DOP (PDO: Protected Designation of Origin) status since 1996; it has always been a natural cheese, made of fresh ewe's milk from free-range flocks and cured at least 70 days but aged for as long as 5 months as a table cheese and 8 months and more for grating as an indispensable complement to a great number of first courses. Chipped *pecorino romano* is excellent accompanied by fruit or honey.

INDEX